A GERMAN TEXAN IN WORLD WAR II

WILLIAMS-FORD
TEXAS A&M UNIVERSITY
MILITARY HISTORY
SERIES

A GERMAN TEXAN IN WORLD WAR II

THE DIARY, LETTERS, AND MEMORABILIA OF AN 88TH INFANTRY OFFICER

Marilyn Melcher Maddox

Foreword by John A. Adams, Jr.

TEXAS A&M UNIVERSITY PRESS
College Station

First edition

∞ This paper meets the requirements of ANSI/NISO Z39.48-1992 (Permanence of Paper).
Binding materials have been chosen for durability.

Library of Congress Control Number: 2025009981
Identifiers: LCCN: 2025009981 | ISBN 9781648433320 (printed case) | ISBN 9781648433337 (ebook)
LC record available at https://lccn.loc.gov/2025009981

This memoir is dedicated to all US Armed Forces,
those living and those who have passed on,
with undying gratitude for their service.

The names, places, and dates of our country's past can be found in books, scholarly journals, and elsewhere. The very hearts of Americans, though, can best be found and felt in memoirs such as this. It is hoped that this book will inspire others—veterans and indeed all parents and grandparents—to preserve their memories for future generations.

This is the day and the hour for us. It's the thing every soldier always has way back in his mind from the day he first puts on his uniform. You feel the tenseness, the waiting, and the anxiety in the air. You feel the bigness and the terrific importance of your job. And then you think of the things most dear to you—the real things that count in your life. And then you feel closer to God than ever before—and you pray for success. The time now is in minutes until we attack in the face of death.
In just one minute. It's on.

—*Robert L. Melcher, May 11, 1944*

CONTENTS

FOREWORD

Robert Lee Melcher

JOHN A. ADAMS JR.

The experiences of Texans during World War II are rich and varied, filling volumes with their stories. Thousands of Texans swiftly donned uniforms after the attack on Pearl Harbor. Similar to the hesitancy felt before the First World War, many individuals in Texas and across the nation were initially wary of being drawn into another European conflict during the late 1930s. However, once the war was officially declared, Texans answered the call of duty.

Among the most distinctive groups were the German Texans: mainly third- and fourth-generation immigrants who had deep roots and strong ties to the Lone Star State. These new Germans in Texas had left their homeland for a singular reason: the fear of being drafted to fight in someone else's war. Once in Texas, their German heritage and determination played a crucial role in taming the frontier and establishing order in their new land, leaving an indelible German imprint on all aspects of their Texan homes. In Texas, they forged a path toward a free and independent future.

Beginning in the mid-1880s, a unique blend of native "Deutsch" and English spread across Texas. This linguistic fusion gave rise to a distinct German Texan accent that persisted well into the 1950s. Despite this linguistic tapestry, these individuals were unequivocally Texans and Americans. Among those who had arrived at Galveston from the old country were the Johann Friedrich Melcher family from Preussisch-Minden, Germany. Settling at La

Grange along the Colorado River, they became an integral part of the German colony in the Texas Hill Country.

The heart of this narrative lies in the wartime experiences of Robert Lee Melcher. Growing up in a traditional German household, he didn't speak English until the first grade, though he quickly adapted. However, the aftermath of the First World War and lingering anti-German sentiments led to a shift. Speaking German in public was met with disapproval, yet within families, it thrived. In 1928, Bob graduated from La Grange High School and embarked on a new chapter at the A&M College of Texas, Class of '32. German-trained faculty and students of German heritage from across Texas had been an integral part of the college since it opened in 1876. As a member of the Corps of Cadets, Bob gained his initial exposure to military life and preparation for the journey ahead following graduation.

Commissioned as a lieutenant in the Army Reserve, Bob continued at A&M for his graduate education. In the mid-1930s, he married and pursued a career as a teacher and an agricultural economics adviser. But everything changed in early 1942.

I met Bob in the mid-1970s, though he was known to me at the time as Colonel Melcher. His stories from his cadet days in the early 1930s always fascinated me, but what truly intrigued me were his reflections on service as commandant of the "fish"—the freshmen—during the postwar years at the Annex, now known as the RELLIS Campus. The bustling main campus had relocated the freshman cadets to the old Bryan Air Force Base because of the surge of veterans returning to school after the war. After this, Bob took on the role of counselor for the Corps of Cadets during the 1950s, followed by other duties including civilian student counselor and foreign student adviser.

Oddly enough, we rarely delved into his wartime experiences, a fact that I now deeply regret. I miss his firsthand perspective, his dry wit, and his wisdom. Thankfully, this volume, meticulously compiled by his daughter, Marilyn, fills many of the gaps I missed. Through her work, we gain insight into Bob's wartime memories—captured in letters, diaries, and memorabilia—as she and her father sifted through those old, dusty boxes of treasures saved long ago.

In all, this stands as a fitting tribute to a remarkable Texas Aggie, Robert Lee Melcher, and to the sacrifices made by his generation of Americans: a legacy that forever changed the world.

PREFACE

Growing up as the daughter of a colonel in military intelligence was an adventure, and it was an adventure to write this memoir, too. It took me sixty-plus years.

My journey into the World War II of my father began in the summer of 1962 when Dad opened an old ammunition case to show me its contents. My interest in the war was ignited. Living in an area defined by military influence and academia, I grew to love hearing Dad's occasional war stories, and I eventually went on to study and then teach American history.

I learned that relatively few World War II books, among thousands written about American involvement in the war, capture first-person accounts of German Americans. Even fewer tell of German Texans who fought against the Fatherland. *A German Texan in World War II: The Diary, Letters, and Memorabilia of an 88th Infantry Officer*, full of researched and confirmed details, tells such a story.

My father, Col. Robert Lee Melcher (Reserve, Retired), was a proud Texan and a loyal American, yet he was also a full-blooded German. With the advent of war, could he resolve his strong German background with fighting against the Fatherland? He reported to active duty as a first lieutenant, progressed to captain, and eventually became a major during the war. As the war progressed, being fluent in German, my dad occasionally interrogated German prisoners and deserters. He learned firsthand what they were experiencing, from their point of view. He also witnessed the enemy's cruelty and saw a different side of the German traditions and pride that had molded him as a youth. He wrote on May 3, 1945, "I'm sure the pictures and stories of German prison camps [POW camps] are convincing as to the true nature of Germans. And convincing as to what the US would have been in for, had we not fought when we did. My idea of a German is lots different than what it was. Some of my friends were in those camps."

Dad served as a US Army major in North Africa and Italy and, a prolific writer and keeper of records, faithfully wrote in his war diary, which was unseen by censors. He also wrote about his experiences in letters, many letters, and his loved ones seemed to sense their historical value and saved them. Dad sent home—and saved in his footlocker—countless items of memorabilia as well. Years after the end of World War II, I discovered, secreted away, Dad's memories of battlefields and command posts. I opened dusty cardboard boxes holding my father's diary and letters, still with their yellowed envelopes. I emptied crates full of scrapbooks, hand-drawn maps, propaganda sheets, medals, and more.

When I opened Dad's boxes of memorabilia, I was overwhelmed by the wealth of primary and secondary sources inside. Never had I seen so many relics from the war, outside of World War II museums I had visited. Always the educator, I recognized the importance of these items to building Dad's memoir and, later, in becoming part of an exhibit. I knew that, just as Dad's war diary should be shared, so too should the memorabilia he had saved.

All of the images in this memoir are of the actual artifacts my father saved from the war. Great care has been taken to verify places, names, and dates included in my father's war diary and letters. Often my father mentioned soldiers' names, but sometimes only their first names. Wherever possible, though, I inserted the soldiers' full names, when I could confirm them, into the diary and letters in brackets. Sources of newspaper clippings have been credited wherever possible. Sadly, though, many clippings in my father's collections were pasted into scrapbooks those many years ago such that the bylines or sources were obliterated or omitted entirely. This, unfortunately, made it impossible to identify them and seek approval for their inclusion in this book.

The writing in my father's war diary and letters has been edited only as follows: minor corrections such as punctuation and rewording where needed for clarity, and occasional omission of very personal or sensitive details.

The places, names, and dates of our past can be found in books and on the internet. The very hearts of Americans, however, can be found and felt in memoirs such as this. Perhaps this memoir will encourage you, too, reader, to delve into and record your own family's history.

This is Dad's story.

A GERMAN TEXAN IN WORLD WAR II

Introduction

The Journey Begins

Summer 1962

"Come look at what I've found!"

"Rats." As much as I had tried to play unnoticed, Dad must have heard me. I glanced toward his voice. From his tone, I knew I wasn't in trouble, but I figured I would be asked to help with some boring chore. Slowly brushing the dirt off my knees, one knee at a time, I whispered farewell to my afternoon's playmates. My masked Lone Ranger and his faithful sidekick Tonto would just have to wait. Reassuring them that I would return, I propped them next to their plastic horses at the edge of our asphalt driveway. I sighed and dragged my feet as I headed back to our garage. Surely Dad wouldn't ask me to help him with his latest project? I was an eleven-year-old tomboy enjoying the freedom of my Texas summer, and I had better things to do than pack up and move dusty old boxes around under my father's watchful eye. After all, summer would end soon and school would start again, so I had very few minutes of fun left to waste.

My dad had been convinced that day (finally, according to my mother, who was experiencing one of her routine cleaning binges) to clean out the jumbled closet at the side of our one-car garage, and he had been sweating through it for several hours. Reaching the garage, I held my breath and peeked around the door, barely moving, hoping that Dad wouldn't notice me and had forgotten that he had called me. I saw black-and-white photos littering the floor and tiny specks of dust drifting lazily through the stifling air. Faded magazines and books had been stacked on the concrete floor around my father, next to piles of scrapbooks, folded maps, and other old items. Cardboard boxes lay open, waiting to be filled and labeled with his careful, distinctive lettering. Why would he want to save all this old stuff, anyway?

He saw me, of course, and pointed toward two or three small, rectangular cases. Their olive-green metal bore faded yellow stenciling. Each metal case seemed sturdily clamped, as if something important had been packed inside.

"Bet you can't guess what these are! Let's take a look at what's inside."

Treasure? I was hooked.

Dad always knew how to capture my interest. He carried the securely clamped metal containers to our backyard, and I followed closely behind. Sitting on the St. Augustine grass under the shade of our towering oak, he said, "I had almost forgotten about these." He hesitated a minute, looking off into the distance, and then pried open one of the cases. He told me that these were old wartime ammunition cases.

For some reason I didn't know at the time, he had long ago packed a few unopened wartime K rations inside. He lifted out some of the tins and packages.

I'm sure he knew what would come next.

"Let's open one!" I begged.

My mother must have been watching us from the raised kitchen window nearby. As soon as Dad opened one of the tins and lifted it to my nose for a sniff, we heard her call out, "Robert, don't you dare let Marilyn get anywhere close to that stuff. It'll make her sick!" She was always worrying that something would make me sick. Of course Dad would not have let me actually taste the dark goo inside, even if I had wanted to. I held my nose. He explained to me why this goo smelled so sickly sweet. War rations for the troops were produced as highly condensed foods—and these were pretty old, to boot.

Amazingly, I can still smell that goo today.

That afternoon in 1962 was the first time my dad had actually shown me anything that came from World War II, much less told me anything about

An ammunition case starts it all. I found this case in Dad's boxes of memorabilia.

the war. Up to that point in my young life, I had caught—surreptitiously, I might add— only a few scattered bits and pieces about his wartime experiences in North Africa and Italy. Some nights I crouched deliciously behind the bookcase in our living room, straining to hear the adult voices in the den nearby. After Mom had safely tucked me into bed, I would creep back from my bedroom to listen to my dad—now The Colonel—exchange memories with his war buddies. My dad and my "uncles" would talk late into the night, and the stories that Uncle Jack, Satch, Charlie, Max, and Vic shared with Dad thrilled this young person's ears.

Living in a small town full of military influences, I was accustomed to seeing uniforms. I loved seeing my father in his US Army uniform when he had Reserve meetings and duty, and I particularly enjoyed going to Fort Sam Houston when he had duty there. Eventually I began to wonder what had really gone on in the war. I wanted to learn more about what my father had done as a "real" soldier. Maybe he had fought just like John Wayne or the other heroes I watched at the Palace Theater most Saturday afternoons. Dad must have finally decided that my age of eleven was old enough to start hearing a few reminiscences about his time in battle.

And so began the war experiences that my father would share with me for the rest of his life.

Growing up—disregarding the brief semirebel years of my hippie fascination—I enjoyed hearing Dad's occasional memories about the war, and sometimes I asked to hear more. He usually encouraged my curiosity and answered most of my questions.

I knew that my father was proud to have fought for our country. Still, from an early age, I had known that he had been born full-blooded German, his family having immigrated to Texas from Germany in the 1840s. Sometimes I wondered just how much my father, his parents, and his grandparents had identified with Germany during the war. I knew that the Nazis were "bad guys," but *my family was German*, after all. As a sensitive only child, I worried that some of my classmates would have been told by their parents that Dad was German. Not wanting him or me to seem "different," I never talked about my background with any of my friends. One incident with a classmate that stands out in my mind occurred when I was in the fifth grade. We students looked forward to our turn to be assigned the end-of-day task of folding the American flag. I couldn't wait until it was my turn for this honor! As our teacher called me to the front of the schoolroom, a classmate (dare I say bully?) called out, "Don't let Marilyn touch the flag! Her dad is a Nazi."

Occasionally I worried about my father's feelings about his German heritage. Had it been hard for him to fight against the country of his ancestors? Whenever I approached the subject, Dad's answers to such questions were firm.

He was American, by golly, living the very freedom for which so many had fought. And he never let me forget that I was living that freedom, too.

All-American we were. Fireworks on the Fourth of July, backyard Texas barbecues, New Year's Day sparklers, and all the other trimmings of postwar America were ours. Our little family of three—Mom, Dad, and I—pledged allegiance and sang to our country with pride. We watched and discussed the nightly news when Dad came home from work. We caught the latest war movies, of course rooting for the Allies. I enjoyed my American history and government classes in school, and our family often visited with Dad's war buddies who had relocated to our town. One of Dad's closest college friends—"Satch" Elkins—had fought in Italy as well, and we celebrated every Independence Day at each other's College Station homes.

We had great times with Dad's younger brother Max (Dad called him "Bud"), Aunt Helen, and especially my cousin Max David when they came to visit us or when we saw them in Houston. Life was full with football games on the nearby college campus or in the front yard, quail and dove hunting, fishing, childhood games, harmless pranks, and holidays.

Oh, the holidays! Americans we were, yet our holidays and home life were shaped by our family's German traditions. My cousins and I simply accepted as normal that our parents, grandparents, aunts, and uncles could speak German. Our grandmothers in particular frequently spoke a mixture of "Englisch" and Deutsch, and I loved hearing my grandma talk in her special German Texan dialect. When she warmed up to a topic, she could really go to town, especially holding forth on the old wooden wall phone when she was discussing life with one of her sisters. She gave sips of beer to us grandkids, she butter-fried noodles, and she made kolaches for her kaffeeklatsches on special days. We were served cold boiled cow tongue, potato salad, and homemade bread and pickles for special lunches. And didn't everyone eat sauerkraut with their Thanksgiving turkey or sing "Stille Nacht" before opening Christmas presents?

Dad loved telling stories about growing up as a German Texan and going to college. Through the years, though, even with occasional war stories my father told me, Dad rarely showed me any of what were surely the most important relics from his time in World War II. Why not? He had saved so much!

Dad's wartime diary, letters, photographs, maps, and more had been secreted away . . . waiting.

I discovered them years later.

CHAPTER 1

Family Background, from Germany to Texas

"... as American as anyone"

Looking back, I find it difficult to believe that summer day occurred only seventeen years after the close of World War II. How could I have known that my own journey back into that war—and to the confirmation of my father's legacy—would begin that day in 1962?

At the time, my father was a colonel in the US Army Reserve. He was on staff at Texas A&M College—later renamed Texas A&M University—in College Station, Texas. My father, Robert Lee Melcher, had been born at home in La Grange, Texas, on December 18, 1910. His parents, Max Ernest John Melcher (b. 1882, d. 1936) and Annie Sladczyk Melcher (b. 1884, d. 1978), were part of a very close-knit group of German Texan families whose ancestors had immigrated to Texas in the 1840s.

In the mid-1800s, most German immigrants landed in Texas at the ports of Galveston or Indianola, the latter having been the designated destination for the Society for the Protection of German Immigrants in Texas. This society, known in Germany as the Verein zum Schutze deutscher Einwanderer, was also commonly called the Adelsverein. It had been formed in April 1842 in Germany to foster economic relief for predominantly middle- and lower-class peasants and to support large-group immigration to Texas. It was created by twenty-one German noblemen as a grand endeavor with the ultimate purpose, some claim, of establishing a New Germany in Texas. One of the leaders of the Adelsverein who brought immigrants to Texas was John

Meusebach, and it was he who signed the certificate granting 640 acres to my father's ancestor in the Fisher and Miller's Colony.

German immigrants settled a large area known as the German Belt, which encompassed south-central Texas, stretching from parts of the Texas Hill Country in the west to Houston and Galveston in the east. These early German settlers expected that the Texas coastal plains and the rolling hills of Central Texas would be ideal for settling and raising their families. They were promised virgin forests, plentiful game, rippling creeks, and fertile lands that begged for their crops. The immigrants had not known, however, to expect the various hardships that awaited them: long and difficult treks toward their new settlements, insufficient supplies, and numerous illnesses such as dysentery. As they made their torturous way inland, the Germans encountered Texas heat and humidity, mosquitoes and wolves, and occasional marauding bands of Comanche. Many of their destinations lay in the hunting and raiding grounds of the Comanche and Tonkawa tribes, who viewed the immigrants with occasional disfavor. These determined pioneers knew what they had left behind in Germany, though, and they knew what they were heading toward: opportunity and freedom in a glorious new land—Texas!

My father's great-grandfather Johann Friedrich Melcher (b. 1813, d. 1892) came to Texas in 1846, most probably landing at Indianola. Family records indicate that he came from a German area called Preussisch-Minden at the time. As his family traveled inland from the Texas coast to join a German settlement that was part of the Fisher and Miller's Colony, their journey was delayed at the Colorado River because of flooding. They waited in the small town of La Grange for the floodwaters to recede and for the ferry to be available again for crossing. Settled around 1819, La Grange was proving to be a growing community and a good stopping point for those traveling to Central Texas. A fort had been built there in 1826 to protect settlers from Indian attacks, and the community had grown up around Moore's Fort. Platted in 1837, the little town of La Grange welcomed the German immigrants.

While the Melcher family waited for the river to go down, Johann Friedrich spent his time making chairs, tables, buckets, and drinking dippers out of the cedar that was so plentiful in the area. Such items were useful to local residents and to soldiers stationed at Moore's Fort nearby. When the floodwaters finally subsided and the ferry across the Colorado River again commenced operations, the locals persuaded him to remain in La Grange to continue his carpentry and woodwork.

One of his children, my father's "O'Pa"—German for "Grandpa"—was born in a log cabin in La Grange near that same Colorado River. John Charles Melcher (b.1849, d. 1941) grew up to be a creative, industrious store owner, farmer, and inventor. While he kept his store stocked and running, he helped manage the family's ten children and took out patents with the US Patent and Trademark Office for his inventions.

Johann Friedrich Melcher, the family patriarch who immigrates to Texas in 1846, is shown here in old age in La Grange, Texas.

Above, Surrounded by his large family, John Charles Melcher is a storekeeper whose inventions include a honey extractor and an adjustable-height table.

Facing, Dad's parents, Max E. J. Melcher and his wife, Annie, both German Texans, continue many traditions of the Old Country in La Grange.

O'Pa loved to tell his grandchildren—including my father—about one of the most exciting events in his life. This occurred around 1861 when he was about twelve years old. At this time in Texas, many men were being sent to fight in the Civil War. This left fewer able-bodied Texans to defend their homes against raiding bands of Indians, mainly the Comanche and their allies. Young O'Pa had been sent by his mother into town on an errand. Around noon, he stopped at Buckner Creek near La Grange to let his horse drink. As he sat resting on his horse, his mount suddenly jerked up her head from

the creek. Just then, he heard Indians galloping toward him, shouting and waving. He heard their shouting but thankfully no shooting. Knowing that Indian raiders sometimes kidnapped healthy young farm boys for adoption into their tribes, he feared they might capture him. He raced toward the Colorado River ferry and safety. Fortunately, he was on a fast horse. In town later, being a well-behaved son who did not like to get into trouble with a strict mama, he went about his chores and prepared to head home. He sure feared riding the same route back to their home outside town, though. This is but one of the stories often retold at Melcher family reunions.

Throughout their early years in Texas, these German immigrants clearly experienced physical and economic hardships, Native Americans, and the Civil War, and they supported each other in building their new lives in Texas. While becoming Texans, they also held on to much of their language and dialects, culture and beliefs. Most continued to live close to their families, with few moving to other locales until the mid-1900s. To this day, German enclaves still exist in Texas, particularly in the Hill Country. Today's descendants of the early immigrants can still be heard speaking German Texan, with a gentle yet noticeable German inflection. As late as the 1970 census, 58 percent of Gillespie County residents claimed German as their mother tongue. Fredericksburg (in Gillespie County), Boerne, New Braunfels, Schulenberg, Weimar, La Grange, and other towns continue to bear remnants of their German roots.

Growing up in the small rural community of La Grange in the early 1900s, Robert Lee knew well the dialect and culture of his German family. Robert Lee, his younger brother Max Allen, and many of their school friends had a pony, a gun for hunting, and several faithful bird dogs as companions on their adventures. After chores at home, of course.

It was only in first grade that Dad formally learned English. Until then he had spoken only German, peppered with a few English phrases, at home, with his friends, or in town. At this time, though, openly speaking German was becoming frowned upon, or even banned, in some locations across the country. Anything German, indeed anyone simply uttering the German language, was causing alarm among the citizenry. Only English was to be taught in American schools, and in classrooms and at recess, children were forbidden to speak their language from home. In Texas, state law in 1909 and again in 1918 established English as the official language to be taught and used in public schools.

Under the expanding shadows of World War I (the Great War of 1914–1918), intolerance reared its head in America. Americans were turning suspicious eyes toward their German American neighbors. In addition to increasing school restrictions, German singing groups and heritage clubs called the Verein were disbanded. Lutheran churches and similar denominations were banned from preaching in the German language. German homes were raided, libraries were forced to remove German books from their shelves, and whippings and beatings were inflicted upon German Americans in some areas. In 1917, a Catholic priest who was a recent immigrant to Texas from Germany was tarred and feathered. Not just Texas but also Illinois, Ohio, Pennsylvania, and other states with large German populations experienced such intolerance.

One of my father's early boyhood memories took place during World War I. Anti-German sentiments were occasionally expressed even in his small hometown of La Grange—curiously, considering its large number of German and Czech residents—and resulted in a few raids of German Texan homes in the area. My father's family home was raided one night. A small child, Dad crouched hidden in the back of a kitchen cabinet, hushed by his mother, when an unruly group pounded on the family's front door. Some local residents had suspected that their German Texan neighbors were hoarding sugar and other difficult-to-find commodities. This mob soon left the Melcher household empty-handed, though, food shortages and the family's solid American patriotism being what they were. Crawling out of the kitchen cabinet came a confused little boy wondering why some people didn't like his family.

Such a memory as this, however, did not dampen my dad's developing love for the country of his birth—and his growing conviction that he was just as American as anyone.

World War I ended in November 1918 when Germany was defeated and signed an armistice agreement with the Allies. The years passed, with my father's immediate Melcher family remaining in La Grange and in a nearby community named O'Quinn. My father graduated with twenty-two classmates from the local high school in La Grange in 1928. Having worked after school and during summers, plus with his parents' support, Dad was able to fulfill his dream of pursuing a college education. He enrolled at nearby Texas A&M College and was one of more than two thousand members of the Corps of Cadets, which was mandatory for most if not all students at that time. Life in the Corps must have been tough because he ran away during his first month of college. He hitchhiked some seventy miles home, and his father promptly packed him up in the family car and drove him back to school. In a German way of speaking, Dad was convinced never to try that again. You finish what you start.

Dad remained in College Station and formed lifelong friendships with many college classmates, some of whom served with him later in World War II. He proudly received his BS in marketing and finance from A&M in 1932. Soon after, he was commissioned as a second lieutenant in the Army Reserve and remained at the college to earn an MS in agricultural economics.

During Dad's college years, Texas A&M was predominantly an all-male school. Dad and his classmates relied on finding dates among the young women who lived locally or who came from nearby towns. He met a lovely young lady who was visiting from Houston. Enchanted, Dad married her, his adored first wife, Alice Bleker, in December 1936. Alice Castles Bleker had been born in February 1916, the only daughter of John S. and Ruby Bleker. Much later, at the time of her passing in December 2001, she was residing in Cedar Park near Austin, Texas. According to her obituary in the *Austin American-Statesman,* she was buried as Alice Castles Bleker.

Soon after marrying in 1936, the young couple moved to Auburn, Alabama. Married life meant moving a few more times, too, as my father spent several years teaching, first at Alabama Polytechnic Institute—now known as Auburn University—and later the New Mexico College of Agriculture and Mechanic Arts. He also worked for a time with the US Bureau of Agricultural Economics within the USDA. Life was good, filled with the new marriage, family and friends, hunting and fishing. Naturally, for my father, this good life also included returning to A&M whenever he could to watch college football games from the stands.

Two interruptions occurred, however, to rock this idyllic all-American life: Alice's recurring bouts with illness and America's 1941 entry into World War II.

My father poses in his Texas A&M Cadet Corps uniform, insignia indicating infantry.

Already serving in the Army Reserve, Dad was called to extended active duty as a first lieutenant on March 11, 1942, and soon arrived for training at Fort Benning, Georgia. He was assigned to the US Army's 88th Infantry Division, which had been reactivated from Organized Reserve in July 1942 at Camp Gruber, Oklahoma. Later, at Camp Gruber, Dad was assigned to Regimental Headquarters, 350th Regiment. Active duty meant extensive infantry officer training with the 88th at camps in Georgia, Oklahoma, Louisiana, and Texas. At last, on December 2, 1943, the 88th Division departed Camp Patrick Henry, Virginia, sailing toward North Africa, Italy, and the unknown.

Throughout training as well as the entire war, my father's concern for Alice's physical and mental health weighed on his mind. During training, Dad was able to be with his wife at times, including an extended leave just prior to departing Fort Sam Houston in San Antonio, Texas, for Camp Patrick Henry. During my research for this book, I uncovered numerous wartime letters from my dad to Alice or to his mother concerning Alice's health. I was surprised to find letters and cards written by fellow officers to Alice, inquiring about her health and reminding her to take it easy. Dad must have felt somewhat reassured, though, knowing that Alice lived with her parents or his own mom during much of wartime.

Even though Dad was of German parentage, he was US and Texas born and bred, and no one who reads his wartime diary and letters can ever doubt his love for America and Texas. He expressed pride in his country and firmly believed in the principles upon which America had been founded. His wartime diary voiced his ardent hope that the world would never again face war's devastation, just as it expressed his deep yearning to return home. Dad wrote too of his longings for his family, for a soft bed and a hot shower, for good home cooking and the wildflowers and rolling hills of Central Texas.

As an American officer who spoke German, he was occasionally called upon to interrogate German soldiers captured on the battlefield. He fought in numerous major battles in Italy, such as Monte Battaglia and Monte Cassino, and he was among the very first American soldiers marching through Rome. His diary mourned seeing firsthand the pain and destruction caused by the Nazis' push for worldwide domination. He felt the joy and relief expressed by the Italians when they were liberated.

Certainly Dad fought for a higher cause, for God and country, as well as for eradication of the Nazis. He felt empathy for his fellow soldiers. He pledged

On a day close to leaving for duty, my father appears beaming and hopeful as Alice snaps his photo.

to remember his fallen comrades all his life, to keep them in his heart and to "always fight for honesty and courage and decency—or else I'll feel I'm not doing right by them."

And he certainly used his knowledge of the German language and psyche to fight "those Jerries!"

CHAPTER 2

The War, the Diary, and More

"Dad's story remained for me to discover."

From 1942 to 1945, Dad writes in this diary, recording his personal reflections of battles and the men and women with whom he serves.

With the end of World War I and the 1919 signing of the Treaty of Versailles, the world breathed a deep sigh of relief, anticipating a return to normalcy and a lasting peace. However, humankind would be humankind: global tensions and economic woes eventually grew. Worldwide economic depression hit in the 1920s, and people everywhere looked for a strong leader to end their difficulties. In 1933, Adolf Hitler became Germany's leader, promising the country a return to stability as well as indisputable power on the world's stage. England and other countries began to fear Germany's growing military might, yet their attempts to appease Hitler and quell his push for domination of Europe failed.

In what seemed like a few short years, World War II erupted, commencing with Nazi Germany's invasion of Poland on September 1, 1939. Germany's blitzkrieg on Europe began. While the United States watched closely, it remained officially neutral—for a time. Most American citizens sided with the Allied powers, and their sentiments heightened drastically in a few short years.

The surprise attack on an American base at Pearl Harbor, Hawaii, by the Empire of Japan—an Axis power—made it clear that the United States would enter the war full force. Citing Sunday, December 7, 1941, as "a date which will live in infamy," President Franklin Delano Roosevelt asked Congress the very next day to declare war on Japan. Pitted against each other in this war were the Allies—principally the United States, Great Britain, France, and the Soviet Union—and the Axis powers of Germany, Italy, and Japan.

After Pearl Harbor, America focused on annihilating the Axis threat to worldwide peace. Americans rushed to enlist in the US Armed Forces, and up to thirty-six million men aged eighteen to sixty-four eventually registered for the draft. Some who were already employed in industries related to the war effort stayed behind. Others were deemed unfit to serve for a variety of reasons, such as age or medical disabilities. Many of these civilians found new work in factories or participated in other wartime endeavors. Countless women replaced men in industry, retail, and even sports leagues. They were officially allowed in 1942 to serve in noncombat roles in the armed forces.

Americans back home learned to limit their consumption of goods in order to support the war effort. Rationing of goods and products was officially guided by the Office of Price Administration, created in summer 1941. Almost to a person, Americans willingly rationed such food items as sugar, canned milk, meat, and butter. Considering rationing as a way of life, consumers also learned to do with less gasoline, rubber, silk, and more. Citizens planted Victory Gardens in their own yards, held paper drives, volunteered where they could, and proudly flew their Stars and Stripes. They were encouraged by the government to purchase war bonds, and they did: revenue flowed in. Patriotism grew and thrived coast to coast. The war machine churned. America was united in one cause: WIN THIS WAR.

The war years wore on, and the once-formidable Axis forces experienced increasing losses. At last, spring and summer 1945 brought great hope to Europe and indeed the world. Russia advanced to Berlin in April and May, followed soon after by the Allies. Seeing the end drawing near, with Russian forces approaching his command bunker, Adolf Hitler committed suicide on April 30, 1945. Soon after, Germany surrendered, and peace was declared in Europe on May 8, 1945. Victory in Europe!

Attention then focused squarely on the war that was continuing in the Pacific. On August 6 and 9 of that summer, the United States dropped the world's first atomic bombs on Hiroshima and Nagasaki. Expecting even greater mass destruction to come, Japan surrendered in a ceremony on the USS *Missouri* in Tokyo Bay on September 2, 1945. Newspaper headlines, radio announcers, and movie newsreels loudly proclaimed that World War II was over.

To this day, many historians, students of history, and history buffs consider World War II to be the largest and bloodiest war in the history of humankind. By its end in 1945, the war had extended to most areas on earth, with unimaginable atrocities and an estimated fifty million to eighty million deaths worldwide. According to numerous accounts, some sixteen million Americans served in different capacities in World War II. More than four hundred thousand Americans—civilians and military—lost their lives in the war.

At war's outbreak, American commanders anticipated many of the challenges their forces would face on the battlefield, away from their homes and families. In one seemingly small measure to keep up their troops' morale during the war, the US Armed Forces advocated writing letters to loved ones back home. Doing so, it was felt, would generate more letters to be sent from home back to the troops on the battlefield. When they were able, sometimes weekly or even daily, American soldiers in Europe and the Pacific sent letters and V-mail to their loved ones at home. For many, this was their only way to remember their life away from the miseries of battle. It brought comfort to write, especially as they looked forward to reading all the news from their loved ones back home.

Military and civilian letters, of necessity, were censored. The Postal Service actively read, blacked out, and cut out details of names, places, and dates for security purposes. Sometimes censorship was so thorough that very little was left in a soldier's communication once it reached the United States. What might happen if letters were captured by the enemy, or if gruesome details about the war upset those back home, thus affecting support for the war effort?

While numerous scholars of World War II report that soldiers were officially banned from writing in diaries, for the same security reasons, many still kept such journals. Enlisted men likely hid their personal diaries away from officers' eyes. Officers, too, presumably kept their own diaries in secret.

I wondered, then, why journals or diaries were even available to soldiers for recording their military experiences. The introduction printed in my father's diary, a 1941 edition of *My Life in the Service,* actually encouraged the troops to write:

> Your experiences in the armed forces of your country are your part of living history. By all means KEEP A DIARY! Times without number, historians and writers have found more information of real human interest in the diaries of enlisted men than in the studied accounts of generals and admirals. This book, conscientiously kept, may prove to be the living record of your destiny five hundred years from now!
>
> Because the events recorded in these pages are likely to be the most significant experiences of your life, and the ones most worth remembering, DON'T TRUST YOUR MEMORY! Few minds are endowed with the capacity to recall in retrospect the dates and details of even the most important events. Cherished memories are distorted or lost forever during the passing of the years. The very names of your closest associates and dearest companions may be forgotten.
>
> The value of this record lies in the future; the time for you to create that value is now. The effort required is small, but eminently worthwhile. Resolve to make an entry, however short, each day. As your diary takes form you will come to count as lost that day in which you have not written an account of its happenings. . . .

> And by all means, PICTURES! One picture is said to be worth a thousand words. . . . Get as many pictures as you can, of people and places, for an illustrated diary is the best of all!

Perhaps my father had acquired his diary prior to America's actual involvement in the war, or possibly he had succumbed to an ingenious marketing ploy. Regardless, he must have read these words and taken them to heart. Already a lover of the written word, Dad had kept diaries since seventh grade and so he wrote dutifully in his 1941 copy of *My Life in the Service* throughout his time in North Africa and Italy. Now, so many of the words in this, his memoir, are the very words he wrote in his diary back in 1942–45. Many of his entries were written late at night, some by candlelight or flashlight so as not to waken those sleeping nearby. Some entries briefly recounted the day's planning and actions; some sadly named those who had been lost; others looked painfully inward.

In addition to recording memories in his diary, Dad also wrote letters to those back home. He kept in touch with Alice, his brother Max Allen and wife Helen, his mother ("Moms" or "Ma"), his maternal grandfather ("O'Pa"), and the list goes on. I am thankful that many of Dad's wartime letters remain; most of those in my possession were saved by his mother. When I finally found them in a dusty, long-forgotten box, they were still bundled together, in order by year and postmark date, held together by fragile rubber bands. Envelopes occasionally bore notes in my grandmother's wobbly script: "This letter was written on board ship" was inscribed on a December 1943 envelope, for example.

Dad also kept an almost unbelievable amount of memorabilia. He saved photographs (those "pictures" that his diary had so heartily encouraged), letters from home, and handwritten notes from other soldiers. He saved Officers Club menus, holiday programs, propaganda, and battle maps. Some of the souvenirs he stored in his footlocker, and some he sent home for scrapbooks that he and Alice would put together later when—*not if*—he returned home.

Writing late at night after a day's battle, could Dad ever have imagined that his daughter would read his thoughts so many years later? Did he somehow know that I would one day pore over the very letters and pictures he had treasured? As an adult, how fortunate I was to be able to read his diary entries and discover details that confirmed and added to the war stories he had once told me. I remember as a teenager finding it hard to believe Dad's story about

My grandmother saves stacks of letters sent by my father during the war, and I discover these in one bundle that has been secreted away for years.

starving Italians carving slabs of flesh off horses and mules that lay dead in the streets. Years later, I unfolded a yellowed and worn letter that my father had sent from Italy in which he mentioned seeing this very sight.

Many of Dad's letters described some of the actual items he had received from home. In one letter, Dad wrote to Alice, "I've caressed that package of Texas dirt that you sent me many a time since I've been aboard ship . . . and I intend to carry it with me as long as I am away from our great state."

He did carry that dirt-filled envelope with him, and to this day I can hold it in my hand and shake it to hear the dry soil rattling inside. Dad's words certainly came alive when I first held that very packet, still sealed, still filled with Texas dirt.

I discovered all these memorabilia many years after my dad had packed them away. Even though he had told me war stories, I had never seen his actual diary, scrapbooks, or letters. My dad was a sentimental man; perhaps it would have been just too painful for him to show them to me himself. Perhaps he did not want to focus too much attention on his past battle experiences, his fallen comrades, or his first marriage. Would this upset Dad or me—or my mom, his second wife?

Dad's story of the war remained for me to discover, and it now remains for me to tell. America's past, particularly first-person accounts such as my father's, should not be stored away in dusty attics or crammed closets.

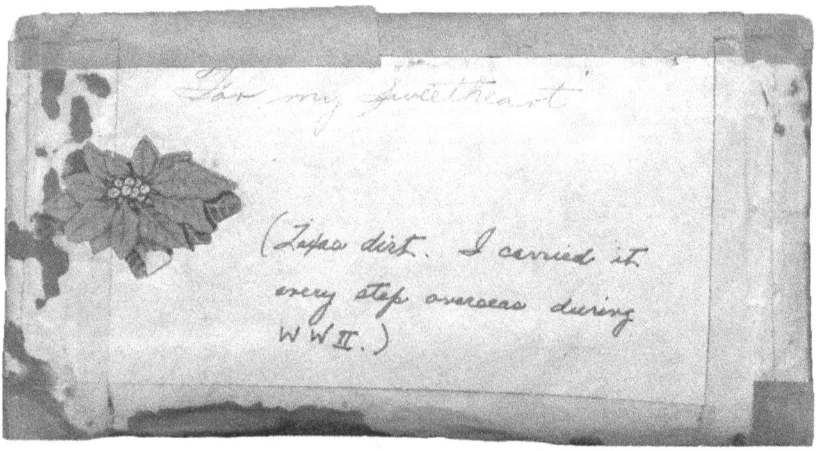

Alice sends this packet of Texas dirt to my dad during the war, giving him hope that he will return home to Texas.

CHAPTER 3

November–December 1943

". . . many an anxious look on the faces of the men. . . . Including mine."

Letter from Fort Sam Houston, Texas, 3:04 p.m., Saturday, November 20, 1943

Dear Moms,

Well, Ma, now I'm sitting here by my desk, waiting for the next train to come in and pull out, and answering a last-minute frantic and occasional phone call. Everything is cleared out of buildings—they are now being inspected—and we're all set.

I'm awfully happy over your letter, Ma; you and Alice have the right attitude toward it all. I can't say I'm happy over the prospect of leaving Alice and you, and Texas, but I'm ready to do my part to help keep this country the great nation it is. I just hope that I'm equal to what I'm called on to contribute.

Take care of yourself and also of Alice for me, Ma. She's a very sweet woman. Make her rest and take things easy when she's with you—promise me that.

Don't worry about me. I'll be back and it may not be as long as you all think.

Love, Robert Lee

P.S. No word of this to anyone yet. But tell O'Pa and everyone hello.

Packed for the train to Camp Patrick Henry, Virginia, my father (left) and "Col. Pete" (middle) appear with an unidentified soldier. Photo is taken at Fort Sam Houston, San Antonio, Texas, November 1943.

Saturday, November 20, 1943

Left Fort Sam at 1945 [7:45 p.m.]. Hope our training has been worth it. Sure had a funny feeling in the pit of my stomach.

Tuesday, November 23, 1943

We are nearing our POE [point of embarkation]. Col. Pete [Col. Charles P. Lynch] is giving 'em hell, making everyone clean up—especially the S-1 [Personnel]. [Capt.] Ray Simpson and I are together on this trip. Hope we are together on the same train headed home when this is all over. Did quite a lot of drinking and poker playing on this trip. Up $2.25.

Wednesday, December 1, 1943

This is our last night on dry land [Camp Patrick Henry, Virginia] for a long time. All packed now—I have time to write in this diary and to send letters to Alice and Ma. We sail tomorrow. Stern and I promised each other that two years from this Thanksgiving we would be back in the [football] stands at A&M. I hope so.

Thursday, December 2, 1943

The first nite [*sic*] on ship—we got on at 1302 today. Now we're anchored a few miles out waiting for other ships to come to this rendezvous. This [the SS *Ward Hunt*] is a Liberty ship—second trip over—the Merchant Marine crew is young and crummy looking. Their pay is way too high in comparison to their work. The ship is very dirty. In this room are the Col., Skalby [Clifford M. Skalby], Yezak [Lt. Herman Yezak], Oresko [possibly Capt. Mike Oreskovich] and I. We also have numerous tanks, planes, trucks and trailers lashed on deck. The men are crowded like rats in one hold. What a target we'd make! There was many an anxious look on the faces of the men as they lined the rail when we pulled away from the pier. Including mine.

Funny feelings: The swing band playing jazz music as we loaded. The feeling in my stomach when we first started to move. I miss Alice and Ma and all the good things in life so much. How I wish we were returning home instead of going to war.

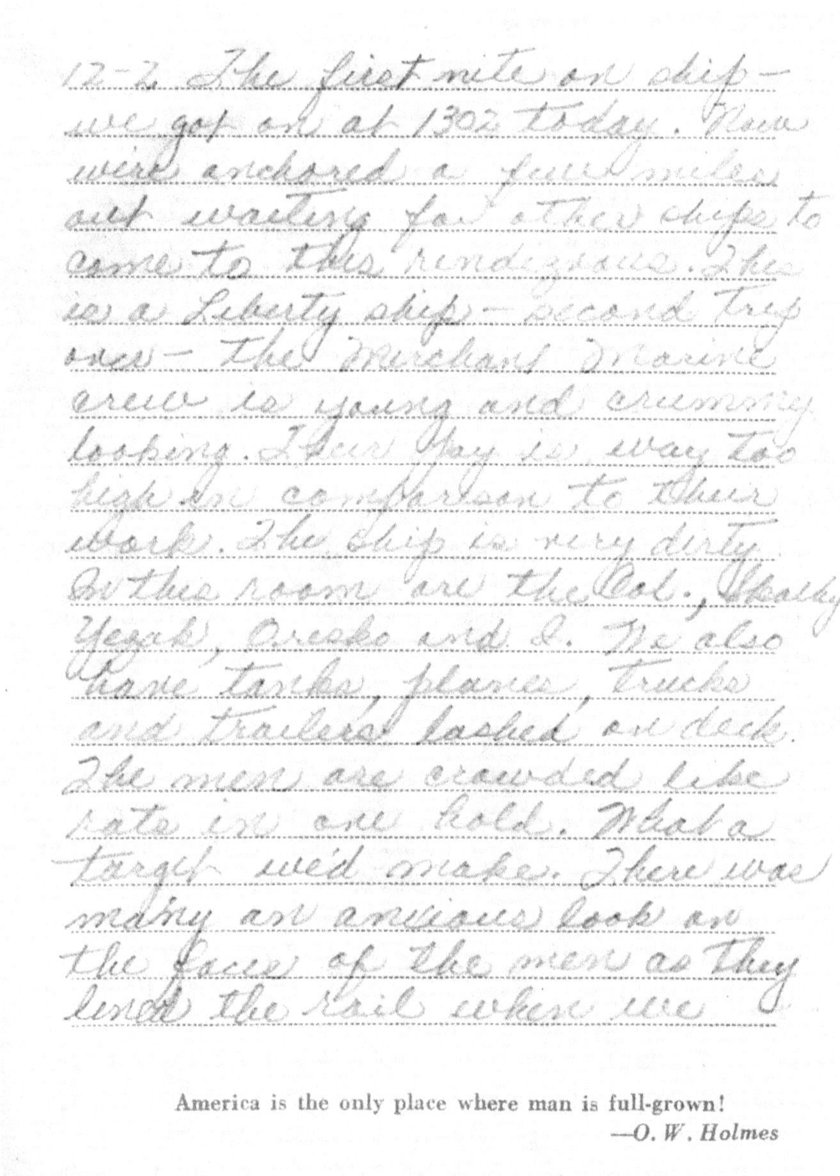
12-2 The first nite on ship—
we got on at 1302 today. Now
we're anchored a few miles
out waiting for other ships to
come to this rendezvous. This
is a Liberty ship—second trip
over—The Merchant Marine
crew is young and crummy
looking. Their pay is way too
high in comparison to their
work. The ship is very dirty.
In this room are the Col., Skalky
Yeask, Oresko and I. We also
have tanks, planes, trucks
and trailers lashed on deck.
The men are crowded like
rats in one hold. What a
target we'd make. There was
many an anxious look on
the faces of the men as they
lined the rail when we

America is the only place where man is full-grown!
—*O. W. Holmes*

In an early diary entry dated December 2, 1943, my dad writes about his first night aboard the Liberty ship that will carry him out to sea, far away from home.

Friday, December 3, 1943

What a mess today! The latrine stopped up (the Merchant Marines didn't give us paper) and the waste dripped through to the EM's [enlisted men's] hold and our kitchen. More and more ships coming out to anchor—part of our convoy.

Saturday, December 4, 1943

Several destroyers came by today, also a big carrier and several smaller ones. Hope they're for us. We actually got under way tonight at 2202—all Officers went on deck. Dark and couldn't see land, waves lapping against the side of our ship. The water looks so black and cold. Wonder when we'll be back. Sure wish I could see Alice and Ma.

Feelings I'll never forget: On deck tonight when we started moving. Not much talking.

Monday, December 6, 1943

We had an alert today. A destroyer up front must have picked up something. Our convoy turned sharp right, then straight again later.

Our quarters are very hot—no ventilation. The EM's quarters are almost unbearable. The Chief Engineer [of the Merchant Marine] didn't even know where to turn on the lights tonight. What a bunch! They claim time and a half overtime for lifeboat drills on Saturday p.m. or Sunday.

Big black jack game every night. Saturday I won $218 and today $93. Got on board with $79.

Tuesday, December 7, 1943

I have a hell of a cold with 101 fever tonight. Practically everyone has a cold—almost no ventilation on this ship. The SS *Ward Hunt* was built for cargo, not troops. We had a real scare today. The rudder broke, all the rest of our convoy passed and we were alone. We were the last ship in row 13 for a while.

Finally the rudder was fixed, and now we're caught up and in our right place, #2 in row 11. We have about 90 ships altogether. Our escort is a converted carrier and 24 destroyers. The sea was really rough today, waves coming over the sides. Not seasick YET, but I went on deck at 0630 today because it was so hot and stuffy. I had to get a breath of fresh air. A cloudy December morn in the Atlantic is sure bleak.

Thursday, December 9, 1943

We're about 270 miles east of Bermuda tonight. Getting in a danger area. Black jack games every night—I've played about four times so far. Did last night until 4 a.m. Then the OD [officer of the day] came in the room as I was crawling in bed and said one of the gunners sighted a sub. Didn't get to sleep until after 5 a.m. On deck most of today. The ocean is mainly calm, but the boat is rocking now. Constant bickering about our meals—the sorriest I've ever had. I must have lost ten pounds since leaving Fort Sam.

Letter from aboard ship in the Atlantic, Friday, December 10, 1943

Dearest Moms and Alice:

Alice, my dear, and Moms, I write this on deck of a ship on a cloudy midwinter afternoon. We are now well on our way to our destination, having been at sea now for over a week. All around me in every direction there isn't a darn thing but water, and I never knew there was so confounded much of it in the world. Of course, plainly visible are also the other numerous ships of our convoy, and in the far distance are also visible some of our escort vessels.

I know that if I were to tell you just exactly how rough the ocean is now you wouldn't believe it—and above all you wouldn't believe that I'm sitting on top of a potato bin typing you a letter. But some of the other Officers sitting around me here on deck have just remarked that the waves are high enough to be level with the deck; that means they are about 18 to 20 feet high. Surprisingly enough I haven't been seasick enough YET to lose my cookies, but I've had that feeling. Every room of Officers has a bet like this: the first one to get seasick pays five bucks into a fund and the last one to get sick in that room wins the pot. I'm going to do a lot of swallowing before I throw money away like that. Ray Simpson [Capt. Ray M. Simpson] has just climbed up here by me and is censoring this letter by telling me what I can and can't write. Ray, incidentally, has looked a little green around the gills at times.

The wind has picked up considerably even in the short time I've been writing. Someone just said the barometer has fallen so much that the liquid has spilled all over the floor. I'm afraid we'll be in for it tonight. I hate nights on a ship. You're stuck down in a little room—five of us—about twelve feet by twelve feet. The ventilation is poor, since this ship wasn't originally designed to be a troop transport, but a cargo vessel instead. And you have a sort of helpless feeling down there in that little room. There's just a little steel wall

Friday, Dec. 10, 2 pm.
Dearest Moms and Alice:

Alice, my dear, and Moms, I write this on deck a ship on a cloudy mid-winter afternoon. We are now well on our way to our destination, having been at sea now for over a week. All around me in every direction there isn't a darn thing but water, and I never knew there was so confounded much of it in the world. Of course plainly visible are also the other numerous ships of our convoy, and in the far distance are also visible some of our escort vessels.

I know that if I were to tell you just exactly how rough the ocean is now you wouldn't believe it - and above all you wouldn't believe that I'm sitting on top the potatoe bin typing you a letter. But some of the other officers sitting around me here on deck have just remarked that the waves are high enough to be level with the deck; that means they are about 18 to 20 feet high. Surprisingly enough I haven't been seasick enough YET to lose my cookies, but I've had that feeling. Every room of officers has up a bet like this: the first one to get seasick pays five bucks into a fund and the last one to get sick in that room gets the pot. I'm going to do a lot of swallowing before I throw money away like that. Ray Simpson has just climbed up here by me and is censoring this letter by telling me what I can and can't write. Ray, incidentally, has looked a little green around the gills at times.

The wind has picked up considerably even in the short time I've been writing. Someone just said the barometer has fallen so much that the liquid has spilled all over the floor. I'm afraid we'll be in for it tonight. I hate nights on a ship. You're stuck down in a little room - 5 of us- about twelve feet by twelve feet. The ventilation is poor, since this ship wasn't originally designed to be a troop transport, but a cargo vessel instead. And you have a sort of helpless feeling down there in that little room. There's just a little steel wall separating you from the water outside and at nights when you lay in your bunk you can hear the waves lashing against the sides, not more than a foot from your head. All our troops aboard the ship are in one big hold at one end. Their bunks are stacked some six high and there is very little space between them. So during the day we keep them above as much as possible, for once darkness falls we observe strict blackout discipline and only officers are permitted on deck.

Now, about 30 minutes later, I'm continuing from our room to which we all had to beat a hasty retreat when a rain caught us on deck. And now I'm beginning to find myself running out of stuff that I can write. Of course there is a lot more I could say but censorship regulations wont permit all those things. Perhaps I can tell you about what we do for entertainment aboard ship. Principally gambling is the biggest form of amusement. Everyplace that you look during the day when training is not going on - and we do have some five hour's training each day- you see poker, blackjack or dice games. The officers never play until night. And everynight there is a big one. I've played about half the times, not any more simply because I've had a heck of a cold and didn't feel like it. However, honey, the few times I did play were right profitable, and if I could get to a p.o. now and buy some bonds, I could almost send you two just like I gave you not very long ago. That sounds pretty good doesn't it?

I've caressed that package of dirt many a time since I've been aboard. Wish I could see acres of it instead. If I get back to the US again I'm going to shoot the person who first mentions an ocean voyage to me. To think that people pay for trips like this in peacetime. I'm very anxious to hear from you all and to have those pictures you and I took that last day, honey. Please don't forget to send them as soon as you can. There is nothing else I want that either of you can send - when there is I'll tell you.

By the time you all receive this letter which I'll mail as soon as I can, the new year will already be here and Christmas time will be over. Never did I dream five years ago that I'd spend a Christmas on water but I guess I will. What a different one this will be from the happy ones we used to spend around our homes. You pay for everything though, I guess, and the dearest things cost the most. At any rate I surely miss you, honey, and you too, Ma. And that goes

In one of the longest letters he writes during the war, Dad describes—with some humor—details about life aboard the SS *Ward Hunt*.

separating you from the water outside and at nights when you lay in your bunk you can hear the waves lashing against the sides, not more than a foot from your head.

All our troops aboard the ship are in one big hold at one end. Their bunks are stacked some six high and there is very little space between them. So during the day we keep them [the troops] above as much as possible, for once darkness falls we observe strict blackout discipline and only Officers are permitted on deck.

Now, about 30 minutes later, I'm continuing from our room, to which we all had to beat a hasty retreat when a rain caught us on deck. And now I'm beginning to find myself running out of stuff that I can write. Of course there is a lot more I could say but censorship regulations won't permit all those things.

Perhaps I can tell you about what we do for entertainment aboard ship. Principally gambling is the biggest form of amusement. Every place that you look during the day when training is not going on—and we do have some five hours' training each day—you see poker, black jack or dice games. The Officers never play until night. And every night there is a big game. I've played about half the time, not any more, simply because I've had a heck of a cold and didn't feel like it. However, honey, the few times I did play were right profitable, and if I could get to a P.O. [post office] now and buy some bonds, I could almost send you two just like I gave you not very long ago. That sounds pretty good, doesn't it?

I've caressed that package of [Texas] dirt that you sent me many a time since I've been aboard. Wish I could see acres of it instead. If I get back to the U.S. again I'm going to shoot the person who first mentions an ocean voyage to me. To think that people pay for trips like this in peacetime.

I'm very anxious to hear from you all and to have those pictures you and I took that last day, honey, that we were together. Please don't forget to send them as soon as you can. There is nothing else I want that either of you can send—when there is, I'll tell you.

By the time you all receive this letter, which I'll mail as soon as I can, the new year will already be here and Christmas time will be over. Never did I dream five years ago that I'd spend a Christmas on water but I guess I will. What a different one this will be from the happy ones we used to spend around our homes. You pay for everything, though, I guess, and the dearest things cost the most. At any rate I surely miss you, honey, and you too, Ma. And that goes for all of our kin folks at home and in Houston.

I guess now everyone is busy with their Christmas shopping, wrapping and mailing packages, and addressing cards. Funny how you miss that—why now I'd even be happy to follow you, honey, through all the stores in Houston, through the mob of people, while you shop hour after hour for a pair of shoe laces. Once I did that, remember? I wonder how Christmas will be in a foreign land. If I can have my feet on dry land, I'll be satisfied.

And then if I can look at the stars at night and know you all can see those same stars, with the safety and hope of a free people who can still wish upon stars, then I'll have a happy day this Christmas. I'll be hoping that other Christmases will find most of us home or on the way home.

Guess I'd better close now before I start dreaming—and that "ain't" good for a soldier. Alice knows how I mean that, Ma. I'll write again before we land, but right now I've put almost everything I know in this letter.

Tell everyone hello, and I don't mind the folks reading this letter. Take very good care of yourselves. I love you. . . .

Bob

Saturday, December 11, 1943

Constant problems with the Merchant Marine. Today I found out that they were using our KPs [kitchen patrol] to make up beds for the ship's crew. I stopped that. Looking forward to tomorrow. I arranged for one can of C rations for everybody. This ship's food is the worst I've ever had. Two meals per day. Seas are very rough today. Waves are coming on deck this evening. We passed the halfway mark today. Golly, I wish I was home with Alice and this was all over.

Saturday, December 18, 1943

My birthday! I hope I'm headed toward home instead of away, next year this time. I'm afraid it won't be, however. Alice's candy that she sent is keeping me alive. The meals are awful, only two per day and usually only soup is for dinner. Haven't eaten but two breakfasts. I read my birthday card over and over today and then wrote Alice.

Monday, December 20, 1943

Nibbling on the little jar of cheese from the rations, right now. I must remind Alice to send more and better cheese than what we are getting. I crave something with flavor. How disagreeable the Old Man [Col. Lynch] is with us today, all on account of a little bar of laundry soap one of us Officers used. We dock Wednesday, so we washed our leggings and web equipment. Guess I will shine my shoes before the first battle comes, just in case the General [possibly Brig. Gen. Paul W. Kendall] is watching. We will pass through the Straits [of Gibraltar] early in the morn so we must be up early. A British convoy joined us today, and we lost some of our own convoy—those going to Casablanca. Sure wish I was home with family, especially for Christmas.

Tuesday, December 21, 1943

Got up early this morn and went on deck. Again it's cloudy and cold and wet. We saw land at 0538: Spain was on the port side and the Atlas Mountains in Africa were on the starboard side. A little later we could see the lights of Tangiers. Things really got screwed up as our convoy passed through the Straits. Boats were jammed up like troops on the battlefield so we just sat for a long time, waiting, making a good target. The crew readied the torpedo net. A tanker loaded with aviation gas cut across our bow and missed us by inches.

I put my foot on African soil for the first time tonight at 8:50 p.m. Collier [Capt. Louis A. Collier, S-2 officer] was on the next ship as we came alongside at the pier. The Colonel [Lynch] and I went with Collier to Ain-El-Turk, to the Officers Club, close to the beach approaching Oran. Had some Herman's Specials. Wham!

After that we drove to Collier's villa. What a place, a summer resort of the rich French on the Mediterranean! Only four Officers in an eight-room apartment! I only had $74 cash for poker, and I owe $150. Others owe me $190.

Things to remember: The mile-long tunnel, the place where the Americans had the casualties, sunken and torpedoed ships in the harbor. This is it—orders today to go to the front in Italy with 15 other Officers for experience. I leave in three days.

Saturday, December 25, 1943

Christmas Day! Gee, I wish I was home. Breakfast and lunch consisted of K and C rations. I had a good turkey dinner with the Colonel, Davis and Collier at MBS [Mediterranean Base Section] Officers Club.

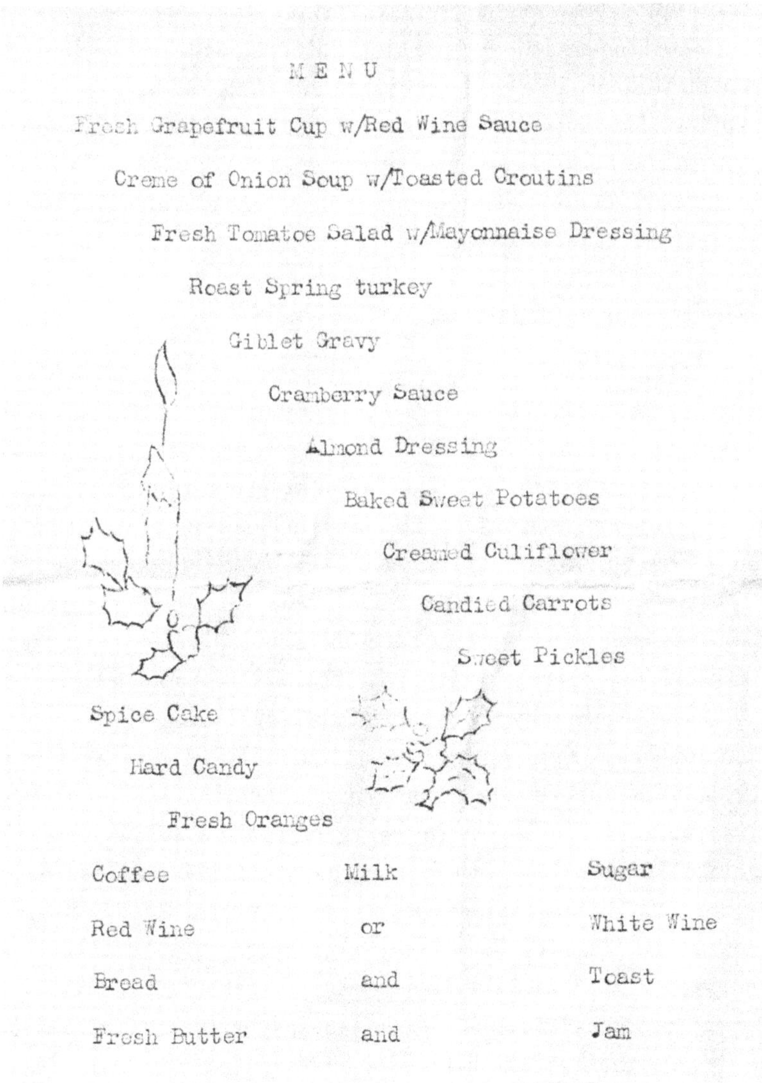

M E N U

Fresh Grapefruit Cup w/Red Wine Sauce

Creme of Onion Soup w/Toasted Croutins

Fresh Tomatoe Salad w/Mayonnaise Dressing

Roast Spring turkey

Giblet Gravy

Cranberry Sauce

Almond Dressing

Baked Sweet Potatoes

Creamed Culiflower

Candied Carrots

Sweet Pickles

Spice Cake

Hard Candy

Fresh Oranges

Coffee	Milk	Sugar
Red Wine	or	White Wine
Bread	and	Toast
Fresh Butter	and	Jam

Christmas dinner 1943 at the Officers Club in Oran, Algeria, features food "just like home" for those who will soon be eating rations on the battlefield.

Last night some of us went back to the club at Ain-El-Turk. I came home first and early. Club again tonight—I got home first at 10:30. Many others brought someone home. We leave for Italy on Monday.

I thought of Alice and Ma and home so much yesterday and today. I can see them around the Christmas tree, opening presents, going to church. Golly, how I pray and hope this war is over soon.

Things to remember: To always be kind and considerate of my fellow man. And to never lose my love for the simple, sweet things of life.

At Division Headquarters in Oran today, noticing how dirty and poor the Arabs seem. The colorful uniforms of the French Colonials.

How I love my country after seeing this place. Never realized before how much was in "Peace on earth, good will to all men."

Letter from Oran, Saturday, December 25, 1943

Dearest Alice:

Christmas Day in a foreign land! I never believed I'd spend Christmas holidays over here—or New Year's either. But you can't tell, can you, honey? Over here you can't see much [*sic*] signs of the holiday season. The Red Cross is the only place I've seen a tree, and today they had some ersatz egg nogs which the Colonel, Collier and I enjoyed. . . .

I hope I always retain that feeling of a real Christmas. I thought of you and what you were doing constantly last evening. And today I know you were at the Christmas tree opening presents. Golly, how I miss you and how I long to be with you—especially at this time of the year.

Right now I can't think of that too much. Let me just say that I love you very dearly and I miss you and home so much. Before we sailed I had six or seven of your letters, and it made me feel good to know you liked those last three months together, too. Boy, weren't they good? I believe they meant a lot to both of us. I'm more in love with you since we were together then than ever before, and I hope it's that way with you.

Well, yesterday I wrote you about going off with a few Officers to another place for some experience. It seems that I'll be able to write you again to-morrow and then I guess that will be all for a while. My dear, of course I know where we're going, but I can't tell you. Just keep the newspaper arti-

During his leave prior to departing for the war in Europe, my dad and Alice enjoy a rejuvenating vacation after Alice's illness.

cles of the current campaigns, for someday I'd like to read them. Remember your promise to me to take good care of yourself. And don't forget above all to love me, for I love you.

Bob

Sunday, December 26, 1943

I moved to another area where all the advance detail is staying. I'm in a tent with Col. Walter E. Bare [Walter E. Bare Jr.], Col. Coleman [Alfred T. Coleman], Maj. Williamson [Corbett Williamson]. Outside it is still raining and very muddy. Company C guard caught an Arab stealing food today. First capture.

Monday, December 27, 1943

Ate breakfast of K rations and Arab wine (vino) and then trucked to the port. Off African soil at 1415, watching Moroccan troops load, also "Ghones"—fierce fighters. They loaded a big ram, dogs, and one prostitute for each of 15 men. Everyone has American equipment. What a drain war is on us! We're on a Greek ship (old *Tuskehanna*) operated by the British, now *NEA Hellas*. Good food! Williamson and I are in one room. About 7,000 troops aboard. I read Alice's letters again—the last one dated November 27. I sure wish I had some letters before leaving for Italy. It'll be a long time now before I hear from home. I sure miss her and everyone at home, Moms especially. But Alice *more* especially.

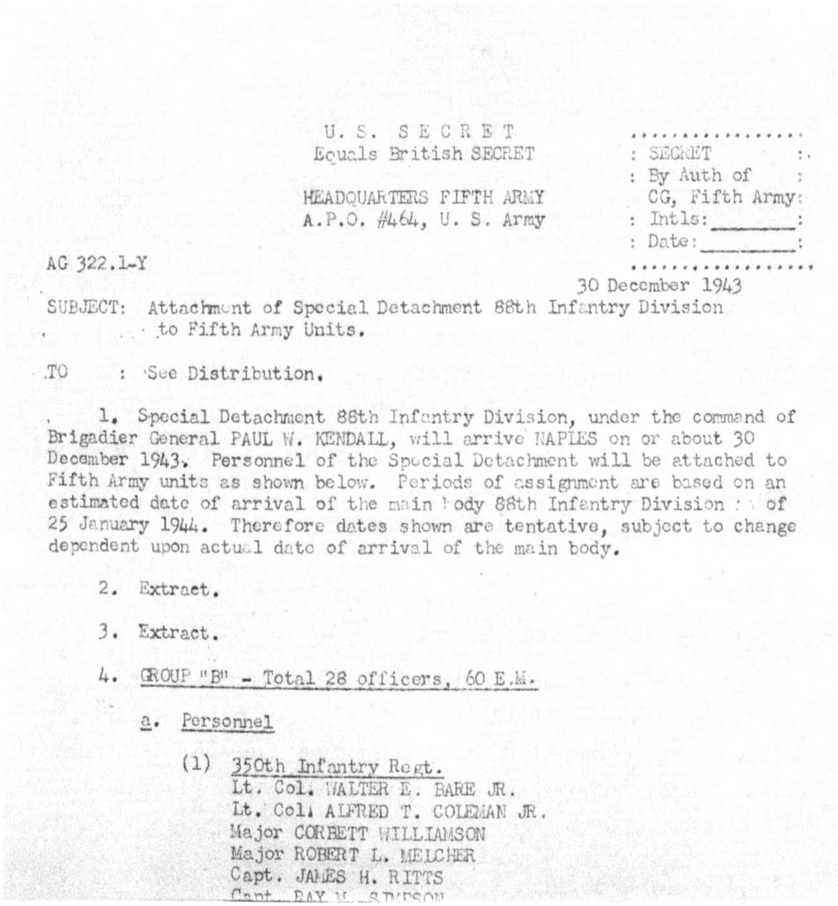

U. S. S E C R E T
Equals British SECRET

HEADQUARTERS FIFTH ARMY
A.P.O. #464, U. S. Army

: SECRET :
: By Auth of :
CG, Fifth Army:
: Intls:_______ :
: Date:_______ :

AG 322.1-Y

30 December 1943

SUBJECT: Attachment of Special Detachment 88th Infantry Division to Fifth Army Units.

TO : See Distribution.

1. Special Detachment 88th Infantry Division, under the command of Brigadier General PAUL W. KENDALL, will arrive NAPLES on or about 30 December 1943. Personnel of the Special Detachment will be attached to Fifth Army units as shown below. Periods of assignment are based on an estimated date of arrival of the main body 88th Infantry Division as of 25 January 1944. Therefore dates shown are tentative, subject to change dependent upon actual date of arrival of the main body.

2. Extract.

3. Extract.

4. GROUP "B" - Total 28 officers, 60 E.M.

a. Personnel

(1) 350th Infantry Regt.
Lt. Col. WALTER E. BARE JR.
Lt. Col. ALFRED T. COLEMAN JR.
Major CORBETT WILLIAMSON
Major ROBERT L. MELCHER
Capt. JAMES H. RITTS

Labeled "Secret," this communication details a special detachment of officers to Naples in early January 1944, the purpose of which is to gain experience.

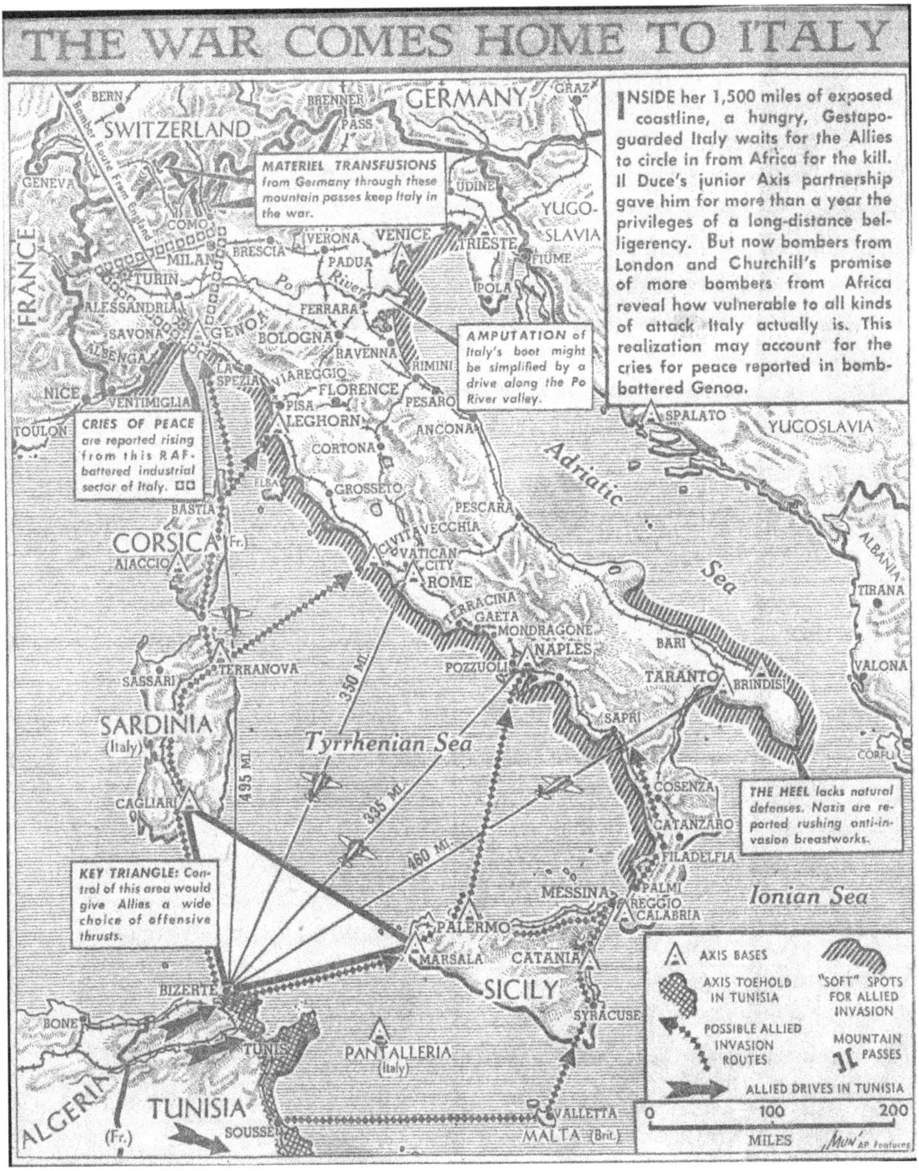

My father saves this newspaper clipping that predicts Allied routes into Italy early in the campaign, 1944. Source: AP Features, newspaper unknown.

Thursday, December 30, 1943

> These are dangerous waters [entering the Tyrrhenian Sea] but we have a heavy escort. Must have about 40,000 troops. We've been talking to French officers and enlisted men plus some Algerian troops. They all seem pretty good fellows. We Americans sound awkward, even funny, using foreign words. The filth in the holds where the Moroccans are is terrible. Many of them have never seen lavatories before.
>
> We gambled last night for diversion, and I'm up about $180 since leaving Fort Sam. I saw some French nurses and WACs aboard. They look pretty good.

New Year's Eve letter from aboard ship, Thursday, December 30, 1943

Dear O'Pa [German for "Grandpa," in this case Dad's maternal grandfather]:

Well, O'Pa, I wonder if you ever thought you'd have a letter from one of your grandsons while he was on the high seas. Right now we're just sitting here in our little cabin waiting for the journey to end. There's not much to do and not much space to do it in. You see, these ships are pretty crowded these days. The water is very calm now and you can hardly tell you're moving.

How was Christmas at home this year? I can remember how much we all enjoyed it when I was a kid and we all gathered at your big house. Those are good memories.

This is all, O'Pa. Tell everyone hello. And I hope you have a very good and happy New Year.

Love from your grandson, Robert Lee

New Year's Eve letter from aboard ship, Thursday, December 30, 1943

My dearest Moms:

I just wrote Alice and O'Pa and now here's a letter to you. I hope you've been able to keep up with me at various times through my letters. . . .

. . . Seems like I've spent half my life on water, and I'll be glad to set my foot on the ground again. And will it be a wonderful feeling when the ground is the USA again.

I had been asleep on my bunk when the other Officer in the cabin woke me to point out a big island. I can see it through a little port hole. It seems very mountainous and the sides drop steeply to the sea. Now if I could see the Statue of Liberty, I'd be pretty happy.

How was your Christmas this year with both of your sons spending theirs in foreign lands? I sure thought of home and all our kinfolks and how we used to gather around the tree and open our presents. Well, it will be a happy one when we're all together again, won't it, Ma?

Take very good care of yourself and tell everyone hello. I hope you have a very happy New Year.

Love, Robert Lee

CHAPTER 4

January–February 1944

"I think the only good thing war brings is the wonderful dream of peace and happiness, and being with the one you love."

Saturday, January 1, 1944, New Year's Day!

I was camped out in the smoking room when 1943 ended. All of the Officers sang, "Should old acquaintance . . ." We were playing black jack for quite a while. Our convoy entered Naples harbor yesterday evening and here we wait. Man, lots of ships are here, and everywhere we can see results of bombing at the waterfront. The city itself seems beautiful, and so does the mountain scenery. Towering Mt. Vesuvius is snow capped and majestic. Picturesque towns hang on the sides of cliffs along the coast. I wonder where my folks are and where I'll be next New Year's.

Sunday, January 2, 1944

We disembarked at 1007 today and then traveled by train to what is called a college, eight miles away. Each of us got our assignments tonight and tomorrow we go up to the front. All crowded in little rooms. Sure is some funny talk going on about what we can expect tomorrow. Well, this is it. May God be with me and guide me.

Letter from Naples, Sunday, January 2, 1944

Dearest Honey:

Well, darling, here we are in Italy—not very far from where there is trouble going on. I'm fortunate in getting to write you as often as I have and being

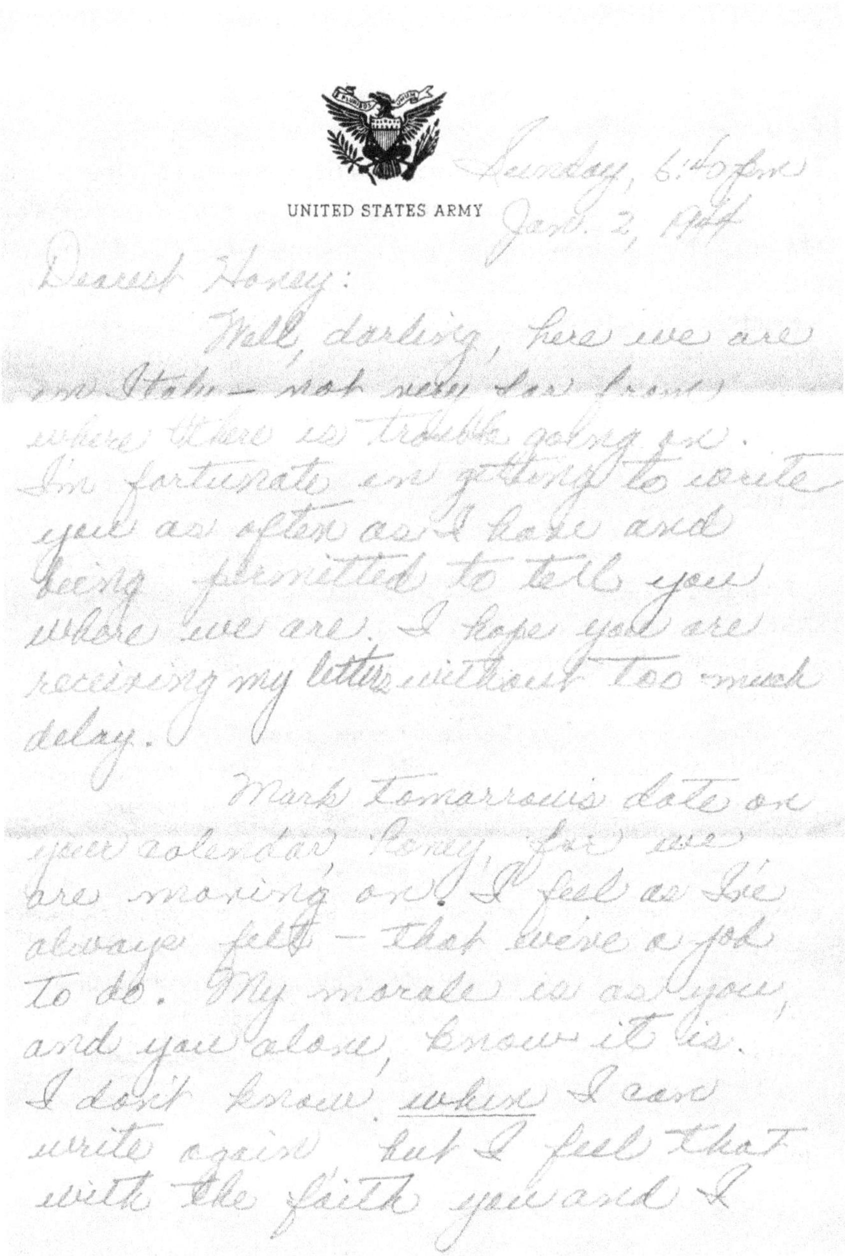
UNITED STATES ARMY

Sunday, 6:40 pm
Jan. 2, 1944

Dearest Honey:

Well, darling, here we are in Italy—not very far from where there is trouble going on. I'm fortunate in getting to write you as often as I have and being permitted to tell you where we are. I hope you are receiving my letters without too much delay.

Mark tomorrow's date on your calendar, honey, for we are moving on! I feel as I've always felt—that we've a job to do. My morale is as you, and you alone, know it is. I don't know *when* I can write again but I feel that with the faith you and I

Dad writes to his wife, Alice, on the eve of moving on from Naples to the front, where he will soon experience his first air raid in combat.

permitted to tell you where we are. I hope you are receiving my letters without too much delay.

Mark tomorrow's date on your calendar, honey, for we are moving on. I feel as I've always felt—that we've a job to do. My morale is as you, and you alone, know it is. I don't know *when* I can write again, but I feel that with the faith you and I have in God, He will let me write again. Take very good care of yourself for me, please, honey. For I'm coming back—back to you and a married life of peace and quiet and happiness. Tell my Moms you heard from me and tell your folks hello for me. Always, regardless of where I am, I'll be thinking of you, honey. You're the sweetest wife in the world and I love you dearly.

Bob

Monday, January 3, 1944

THE DAY. We left for the front at 0810 via truck with 16 Officers and 33 men from our Regiment. To Division CP [command post] and then 168th Regiment where Officers went to companies. It is very cold; muddy snow is in the mountains nearby. Our first air raid occurred at 1515—about 20 of ours were wounded and two killed.

Things to remember: This Regiment is famous—over 5,000 replacements have moved through it so far. Remember how I dove for the fox hole and my feelings as I lay there praying and hugging the ground. How the EMs crowded around their injured and dead buddies. Germans dropping delayed action bombs. Our own artillery firing steadily all around, sounding like tremendous thunderclaps. Good Officers here—I have already learned a lot. How much more than ever before do I wish this war was all over. I hope the Lord stays with me. Very cold and muddy, snow in mountains nearby. People at home just don't realize what war is really like. Our own artillery all around firing steadily—sounds like tremendous thunder. Boy do I wish I were home with Alice!

Thursday, January 6, 1944

Well, I'm still here, and I'm truly thankful. We have moved on up higher in the mountains where it's cold as hell with the strongest winds I've ever felt in my life. Snow mixes with rain, and artillery fires steadily all around us. We're near St. Vittoria; this Division took it today. Our Regiment is moving but slowly. Right now it sounds like a counter attack by Germans on Porchia is starting. Our artillery is blasting 'em. I hope every shell kills a hundred. Funny how you feel when you hear a shell whistling. I saw some of our planes dive bombing and strafing. It's a wonderful feeling when you look up and see our own planes. Boy, will I be happy to get back home and see Alice and Moms and all the folks. I wrote Alice tonight. I'm cold.

Friday, January 7, 1944

What a grand stand seat I had today! I could see an entire front: artillery, dive bombing, strafing, everything. Some German artillery came fairly close, 500 or 600 yards away, but the opportunity to watch overruled my good judgment so I stayed. I still don't see how this one jeep came out of that artillery burst—did he ever take off! Every house in St. Pietro is in shambles, every tree is stripped, shell holes pit every field. Every house is hit and wrecked.

I watched one family sit in the sun and poke through the ruins, and other Italians fixing their battered homes not one mile back of the front lines.

In a photograph taken close to the front near St. Pietro, Italians stand in front of their bombed-out home.

Some Officers from a TD [tank destroyer] outfit came up. One had met Satch [Capt. Rollin "Satch" Elkins, former college roommate at A&M] three weeks ago. His own roommate from college is now Satch's S-2 sergeant. What a coincidence!

We advanced steadily today, moving on Cassino. I was already in bed last night, and a deserter came in. I talked to him but he wouldn't change his mind. I wrote Moms tonight. It's cold as the devil. We were dive bombed again today and I didn't have time to make it to a fox hole—just flopped. Boy, I can really get *flat*.

Tuesday, January 11, 1944

Nothing much has happened. Two or three air raids on Saturday. The fox hole was empty when I started for it—by the time I landed in it, I was the third man there. Days have been cold and muddy. Tomorrow we assemble near Venafro and go to British X corps.

Things to remember: First day in combat, a private taking 19 prisoners. The UP and AP interviewers of the private knew Tony. German morale is low—some desertions, especially Poles and Slavs. Many of them are from the Russian front. The kids always scavenging. The Italian girl they brought to the command post who had been behind German lines. The stories she told us.

St. Vittoria fell and we attack CERVARO today. Counted five or six German artillery duds in the valley right below us about 3 a.m. this morning. Woke me. Scared as hell.

Thursday, January 13, 1944

Glad this 13th is about over, especially since I'm in the 13th Brigade of this 5th Division. These English seem hard to figure out, for me at least. It's not only their speech I can't understand, it's the tea. Tea at 4 p.m., come hell or high water. Their operations that I've seen are not as systematic as ours—so very much talk, sometimes indefinite and vague. I'm wondering how they can get an attack started.

A while back, in the town of Mondagrone [Mondragone], as dirty as any I've seen, we took over some big shot's house, guess it's considered good. It's a rat's nest, bombed out. At least there is a fireplace here. The "batmen" bring hot water in the morn. Linens and silver are laid on the table . . . these English are peculiar. Went to the OP [observation post] today. I won't be in this coming operation. Doesn't look good. We had three air raids in about

25 minutes yesterday just as we left the 168th. I really hit the ground on the second one. I'll be so glad when I'm back in the wonderful USA. I'll never leave it again!

Letter from Italy, Saturday noon, January 15, 1944

Dearest honey:

Suppose I go about it like this in describing the peculiar situation in which I find myself now.

Place: I'm in some terrifically bombed little city in Italy, sitting before a blasted-out window on the second floor of a three-story house—near enough right now to the front to hear the big guns. Down below in the filth-covered streets, not quite ankle deep in mud, are hordes of mostly little children. Ragged, underfed (if indeed fed at all), always begging and following soldiers, always scavenging through any and every pile of filth and rubbish heap, living and sleeping, sitting and lying in any alley, building or goodness knows where.

Where did we get a house, you wonder? Well, the British (whom I am temporarily with) take the rooms they need, and if the family is still at the house and not blasted out of existence, then the family either moves out or lives in the rooms that are left. In back of this house is a grove of lemon and orange trees—every house has those and now they are laden with fruit. The oranges are about the size of a lemon and pretty sour; I haven't braved a lemon yet.

Do you remember the share croppers' houses we sometimes visited in Alabama? They had about the same conveniences that this "better" family had. Except the share croppers were a thousand times cleaner and more sanitary. Of course, that wasn't war time. There is no method of sewage disposal left here . . . the Jerries leave so little of common conveniences behind.

Now for the town: The streets are very narrow for the most part, so a jeep must drive carefully or you scrape the sides of the buildings. The buildings and houses are all of stone or adobe. They are built right up to the street. There is no distinction in town between a house (home) or a building for a business. There are no sidewalks—you walk in the street. There is no yard. Sometimes behind a place there is a little patio where are kept the mules, feed and such stuff. The mules are in reality little jackasses, very small. They are used for everything. The Germans took absolutely everything else. What they couldn't take, they destroyed. This area was, and is, typical of all Italy.

These people are as poor as any in Europe. How the world was fooled into thinking of Italy as a first class power!

Now for the English: I could say a lot which wouldn't get by a censor. But I'll tell you when I get home, honey. Believe me, nothing stops them from their tea at 10 a.m. and 4 p.m. every day. Even troops training out in the field stop their work because here comes a truck carrying tea. They as a whole are friendly and extremely unworried about anything. I have a heck of a time understanding them—there are Irish, Scottish and English in the 19 or 20 Officers I'm living with.

Imagine one Texan at a tea with that "bloody" mob. Boy! They are very formal—dinner tablecloths, silver service, soup first, and someone serves you. Even though the soup is like dishwater and the meat is always canned "bully" [bully beef or corned beef]. They will want America's help badly in the peace time when it comes, to help counterbalance Russia's influence; they want, and are getting, our planes, tanks, guns, etc. They want most everything but I seldom hear a word of gratitude about us coming in the war. (Of course, I still believe we came in at that time to save our own skin.) The sun is out today and I'm glad. So are the 100 million billion flies. Honey, this is the filthiest place you could imagine.

I'll be here about another week, then I'll rejoin my own outfit. At that time I'll mail this. You'll get it faster through American channels than if I mailed it here. Sometime before I see my outfit again the big operation will start and I'll be in it, I guess, getting some more "experience." I've had enough of that; I want to come home to you.

I've time to write this long letter because the main planning work is finished and we're sort of waiting. This is to be a big surprise drive to the Germans—I hope it is. You'll be able to tell by the papers, I guess, of around this date. The town Minturno should be mentioned frequently. . . . You know I believe the only good thing war brings is the wonderful dream of peace and happiness, and being with the one you love. . . .

Bob

P.S. I hope you're keeping my letters. They'll remind me of stuff to tell you when I get home. I am sending a propaganda sheet that we load in our big shells and shoot into the German lines. Let Moms translate it for you, since it is in German so the enemy can read it. Keep it also for our scrapbooks.

DRINGENDE WARNUNG!

Unsere Artillerie gibt Dir von jetzt an keine Rast. Unser Vorrat an Granaten ist unerschöpflich. Du entkommst unserem Feuer nicht. Wenn Du zurückgehst, folgt das Trommelfeuer Dir unerbittlich nach.

Du kannst dem Feuer nur auf eine Weise entgehen: Indem Du liegenbleibst wenn die Anderen zurückgehen und unser Feuer ihnen nachfolgt.

Deutscher Soldat: Wir warnen Dich. Ein Schlag folgt auf den anderen.

Nimm diese Warnung ernst: Wir schiessen Papier nicht zum Vergnügen. Dieser Flugzettel ist Dein Passierschein. Noch hast Du die Wahl — Selbstmord oder Kriegsgefangenschaft. Die Entscheidung drängt. Die nächste Gelegenheit kann Deine letzte sein.

UNSERE NÄCHSTE BOTSCHAFT

GRANATEN!

Some of our propaganda shells. A few Jerries had it too.

Propaganda sheets are shot over to German troops to demoralize them. Dad sends this sheet to Alice, which, loosely translated, begins: "Urgent warning! Our artillery gives you a small rest. Our supply of grenades is inexhaustible."

Thursday, January 20, 1944

I'm sitting in the noonday sun outside a farm house waiting for the British. The operation wasn't so hot. Had a most wonderful breakfast of meat and beans and hot coffee this a.m. I'm tired of tea—it's everywhere. It's absolutely a passion with them, though. Can see Minturno some three miles away. It's ours. We've been watching our planes dive and strafe it. Bombed yesterday. Cut my hand again going for a fox hole. Saw one of our planes shot down—crashed nearby. The pilot had bailed out. Our American stuff is everywhere: guns, jeeps, planes, food. Don't see why we were sent here—learned a flat nothing and that's what the other Americans think too. Sure will be glad to get back to our outfit and get my mail.

Tuesday, January 25, 1944

We're still with the British—it's been almost two weeks now, sweating it out. They can't get over me and my men not shaving daily, yet their messes can be filthy. Our EMs would absolutely refuse to fight on this food, too. In later years, I won't believe all I know and see now. Now in a quarry below Tufa. We are shelled daily—one Jerry battery in particular is bad. Wish they could find him. Saw Gawky yesterday. We both tried for a fox hole at the same time. Shell landed some 60 yards away—killed one Officer and wounded two. The British 1st and American 3rd landed near Rome. Surprise, we hear. Hope they're successful. Sure would like some mail—better yet, to hear the war is over.

Things to remember: The longest 400 yards I ever traveled in my life, under direct fire and observation. He [Jerry] tried for us—one shot short and one shot over.

Also to remember: Questioning the prisoners for this outfit. All Poles—deserters. And one German of 19. They are told the British and Americans would shoot them if captured.

Sunday, January 30, 1944

Left the British on the 26th, to Caserta for instructions and then here to PIEDMONT. All our detachment is here now. Hunter hit by shrapnel—through the helmet and still in the brain. Serious condition. Sure hope John makes it. I like him. We're staying in a school building. No shells here and we're all happy over that. I ate two complete dinners at 5th Army in Caserta. Pitts and Ray traded five cans of C rations for five gallons of Vino. Doesn't taste good. Effective though. Sniped at the last two nights.

Saw the CG [Commanding General John E. Sloan] today.

Excerpt of letter from Italy, Wednesday–Friday, February 9–11, 1944

Dearest Alice:

While I sit here in a pretty nice office in a pretty nice building, here's a little letter. Mike [Oreskovich?] is down here with me, as is Ray and also Gawky, although the latter two are [posted] at another town some few kilometers away. We're doing a little (frankly a lot) of work in preparation for the remainder of our outfit which is going to arrive pretty soon . . . we've been at it for about 40 straight hours.

. . . We're (me and Mike) living in a hotel, which is a middle class hotel compared to our standards, with hot (sometimes) and cold running water and maids. There are some imitation palms sitting in the lobby and last night when it rained they all got watered because the roof is leaking a little from a bombing that took place a couple of months ago. The food here is good and wonderful—in fact, everything is wonderful where it's quiet. The whiskey here is alla, alla, the Italian way of saying there ain't any. But they've got red Vino (wine) by the barrelsfull. We manage to slip in a few little toddies of cognac (no good) or Sarti (don't know what that is) or vermouth (they call it that but it ain't), every once in a while. I guess it sounds like we're having a lot of fun, and we are compared to where we were and what we were up against about a week ago. Actually we're working hard and we know that it isn't going to be long, this kind of life down here in this city.

This place is rapidly opening up its shops and stores, and with so many Americans around all the little junk shops are doing a rush business. The black market is going strong—every corner has its vendors armed with their black market satchels carrying everything from a little piece of precious meat to silk hose.

Later, it's now February 11. Really got a call to go to work as I was typing your letter. Slept about 12 hours since then, hard at it. [It will be] all night tonight again.

Bye, honey, I miss you and love you always.

Bob

Sunday, February 13, 1944

On February 2 Mike and I came down with Col. Pete [Lynch] to Naples to handle details for our Division. Been working hard—all night at times down at the docks in rain and sleet. Very cold. Playing some, drinking champagne mostly. Naples is very crowded. Curfew is at 8:30 and the streets empty out. Where they all go is a mystery.

Things to remember: The bombed post office, the hotel (Parco) we live in, the USOers here, the wallop in 1926 champagne, and how the stopper knocked plaster off the ceiling. We love the peace and quiet and no gunfire, the view over the bay from here and how Mt. Vesuvius glows at night and how beautiful it looked early one morn—snow on the sides, steam rising with the morning sun behind it.

Hope to go to Pompeii today. LATER: We did make it to Pompeii and walked with the ancients today. It will be more interesting to visit in peacetime. No patience today.

Thursday, February 24, 1944

We got the Division in and came to Piedmont yesterday. Collier must have gotten in some good licks. I heard rumors I am no longer S-3. I asked the Old Man about it this morn and he said I was. Very happy over it—my heart is here in S-3 work. Had 48 letters from Alice waiting yesterday. I sure was glad. First mail I have had since November 30.

Good thoughts: The many Officers who were happy to hear I'm still S-3, the warmth with which I was greeted by the EMs and Officers when I got back here. Very cold today.

Tuesday, February 29, 1944

We went down to the British X, the 5th Division, and found we are to relieve the 13th Brigade, the same one I was attached to. What a coincidence! The Colonel and I got in a little artillery, enough to make us jump out of our jeeps. I've been working, still S-3. It's still raining and the mud is ______ deep.

CHAPTER 5

March–April 1944

"God, please make this war with its pain, sufferings and deaths end quickly."

S-2 JOURNAL

ORGANIZATION 350 RCT LOCATION: MINTURNO AREA TIME: from 0600 (hour) Mar. 5 (date) TO: 1850 (hour) Mar. 5 (date)

Item No.	Date	Time Rec'd	Sender	Time Sent	Sent to	Nature of Message	Disposition
1	5		S-3	0515	5th Div	Division notified relief of 13th Brigade completed. 350th now occupies part of 5th Army Front.	
2	5					13th Brigade Hqs. departs at 0555.	
3	5	0700	Blue 6			Mortar burst in Co.L CP wounded 3 men at 0200. Mortar burst on Co.L amm. trail wounded 2 men at 0230.	
4	5	0700	2 Sqn 5th Rec	0530	Div	Report of Night's Activity.	
5	5	0700	"	?		Patrol Intentions.	
6	5		S-2	0815		Request for Location of New Minefield	
7	"		S-2	0830	Div, 201 Art. Grp	Patrol Intentions for 5-6 all units w/overlay	
8	"		S-2		Bns, A-T Can.	Overlay Artillery Defensive Fires	
9	"	0830	5 Div	041230		Planned Air Activity night of 4/5	
10	"	"	"	041530		Withdrawal plan of some Arty. Units	
11	"	1100	"	0800		SITREP/ Relief by 350, Gds quiet patrol contact at 796967	
12	"	1100	201 Gds Brig.	0730		Patrol report	
13	"	1130	5 Div			Intelligence Summary #99	
14	"	1130	"	0930		5th Div. closes here at 1000	
15	"	1500	G-3			Location of Div. CP 925889 1/50000	

This page, from one of many S-2 journals (reports) my dad saves, gives details sent to and received by S-2 near Minturno, including the number of wounded, locations of minefields, and other valuable information for intelligence and planning.

Tuesday, March 7, 1944

Busy as hell. On March 2nd the Colonel and I came to this Minturno front—we're arranging details of relief of the 13th Brigade. Back to Piedmont and the outfit moved to Cascano on the 3rd. Relief took place very smoothly on the night of the 4th. We took over 0515 on the 5th. No letter from Alice in ten days. One from Satch today. He's at Anzio. It's raining all the time, with some sleet. Seems like I'm always in it. Colonel got caught in a concentration today. Wonder I wasn't along. He was very muddy—went under a jeep. Mud is knee deep. Thirteen wounded, two dead so far.

Letter from Italy, Tuesday, March 14, 1944

Dear Moms:

While I wait for news of our night patrols to come in, I'll drop you a line. You know, mail means an awful lot over here. There's so little to write here, but there's so much to tell when I get home. In the meantime, it can wait. We're doing okay—still learning a lot. Guess you always do in a war, though. Believe me, I've done a lot of praying. A fellow prays fast sometimes! Our grub is good—we don't get much sleep—we work pretty hard. It's cold and very rainy here. The mud is up to our knees. Mountains around us are snow covered and my feet are, and have been, frost bitten since about January 10. Seems ages since I left the States. Boy, it'll be wonderful to see Texas again. We get practically no news of the U.S. but that's understood. Mail to the front is pretty good. Our outfit is doing alright. We're getting some Germans and they're getting some of us. We're green, of course, but after the first good shelling you're considered a veteran. Today makes 34 days I've been at the front—some of those days seemed pretty long. But all things can be worse I guess. Maybe you wonder if a fellow gets scared up here. Hell, Ma, I'm always scared. But the Germans are more scared than I am. And that's a consolation, so sometimes you just forget, say a prayer and go ahead on. Maybe it hasn't been long since I left home, but it sure seems long. I miss you and home and Alice and all the folks a lot. But one of these days this mess will be over and I mean I'll be happy to see that great day. Take care of yourself. I love you.

Robert Lee

Wednesday, March 15, 1944

In the command post now just waiting—time to think. You always wonder if maybe you didn't slip, in sending men to a certain spot. Many things have happened; no serial bombings on us yet, but some artillery, some especially close, about 25 feet away. We're making lots of mistakes but we're in a good place to learn. We're mostly patrolling since we've been here. Going out pretty far tonight, and it's raining and black as hell.

Things to remember: Moving through Minturno Castle and all the contraptions around the operation—the generators, our electric lights, the mirrors, furniture, chapel and stuff in the castle. Getting run off the roof by time bursts, and the close one that came in while we were eating. Riding and walking around while the Jerries look down our throats. About March 8 or 9 in a fox hole as far forward as I could get, later picking up Jerries in a house and blasting them to hell. Getting my birthday [which was December 18] package from home on March 13—how good it is to hear from home.

Tuesday, March 21, 1944

Midnight. We are losing too many men on patrols. We've been working on an attack order. If this plan goes through, the CG [commanding general] will make the headlines.

Things to remember: How those bastard Jerries ran me off the latrine the other day. I still have skins and bruises from diving into the dugout. Mortar came in Payer's dugout.

Sunday, April 2, 1944

Midnight again. On March 31 we came back to a rear bivouac area, definitely not a rest area, near CASCANA [possibly Cascina]. Working nonstop ever since. Sometimes it seems like I'm the only one not able to take it a little easy. Of course the S-1 is busy with replacements and everything personnel-related.

The Old Man had recommended me for a Bronze Star but the Division Board turned it down. So today I received a swell over-lavish commendation on Regiment order and a Combat Infantryman badge. Have always been at war with Division staff, and at times the Bull is enough to drive just about anyone nuts. We were relieved by the 339th of 85th. They don't look so hot to me. Sure will be glad when the Great Day comes!

Letter from Italy, Friday night, April 15, 1944

Dearest honey:

Had two eggs this morn, the first over here. These were genuine, not powder. We bought a dozen from a native for $3.00. Money means nothing over here. Goods count; money doesn't. You pay an Italian woman either $4 or $5 to do a little washing or you give her a package of Camels and two bars of soap. Occasional black jack games see Officers betting 20 bucks on a card where in the States they wouldn't bet 50 cents. I do okay. So far. Had quite an exciting time a few days ago. The Colonel and I went on a reconnaissance. It's funny now. We were both pretty close to Mother Earth several times. Never thought I could talk about it in that manner, but you gradually do, I suppose. Can tell you now I was in the preliminaries to Cassino with another outfit and also that prior to March 15 I was with the British when they crossed the Garigliano River back in January. That was a show, believe me! Remember reading [in the newspapers] of the towns Minturno and Tufa? The outfit I was with took them.

. . . I have so little time to think or dream about the pleasant memories, the fun we have had together. Sometimes I wonder if it was real. I will really be glad to get back! Tell my Moms and your folks [the Blekers] hello. Take care of yourself. Write when you can. I love you dearly.

Bob

Friday, April 21, 1944

Well, back at the front! Castelforte is on our right. Colonel Lynch is in the hospital and a replacement from West Point has been with us. After hours, we were off to Naples with Hobson and Fowler of 379th and 350th. At the Orange Club, I saw my British friends sitting at the club. God, please make this war with its pain, suffering and deaths end quickly.

Things to remember: The harassing of us back in the rear area: one button open, $5 fine; no trip ticket, $15. Courts on the spot. The power plant—Ott's Watts, Inc. The black jack games with the Old Man, and when I came to his tent and found four men on the floor with a flashlight to see their cards.

How swell Bill Ott is and what a good guy Skalby [Clifford M. Skalby] is. How Costello [M.Sgt. Francis Costello], a sergeant I work with, anticipates my moods and moves.

Letter from Italy, Monday morning, April 24, 1944

Dear Moms:

Just read your letter in which you enclosed the picture of you by the front gate with old Spot wagging his tail nearby. Well, I'm upstairs in an old Italian house where we have our command post set up. I guess Alice has told you we moved up front again, but don't worry because this is a quiet sector. It's sort of spring here—some of the fruit trees are blooming and some clover is about ankle high. Darn, I can imagine how pretty the bluebonnets and other wild flowers are around home. Where is Vic [cousin Victor Lee Koenig, A&M Class of 1939, later participated in 101st Airborne Division in Operation Overlord, June 6, 1944]? Still in the States? Hope he can stay there.

I read the ads in Life magazine and they portray the glamour and romance of the soldier in the war theater. You just don't see all the glory and stuff in a battle zone. So I hope Vic can stay over there [in the States]. From the stuff I read, the people at home feel the war is over as soon as the invasion starts. That's not the way we feel—that invasion, if it comes off, will be slow, slow and expensive. Our hours now are 5 to 5, so must quit. Tell everyone, especially O'Pa, hello. Take care of yourself and write right away. I love you.

Robert Lee

Master sergeant's patch worn by Francis P. Costello, who serves alongside my father in Italy. Dad keeps in touch with him until Costello's death in 1986.

CHAPTER 6

May–June 1944

"This is what we trained for—I know we're on the right side."

Monday, May 8, 1944

Many days have passed and in the meantime the Colonel [Col. Lynch] came back and straightened out the mess some of the others have caused. And now the Colonel has returned to the hospital [on May 6] with a bad knee. Col. Fry [J. C. Fry] has taken over. I'll reserve my opinion until later.

We're awfully busy on account of the big job coming up, working 16 to 18 hours per day. Well, soon we go off. Please, God, let it be successful and see us safely through it. Gee, I wish I was home.

Things to remember: The shelling while on the ferry. The attack against the 2nd. How swell it is to hear from Alice and Moms. The constant harassing and antics of some of the Division brass. The cockroaches, fleas and rats here in the command post.

Wednesday, May 10, 1944

We're just about through with all the arrangements—a few last conferences tomorrow. I'm just about through, too. Tomorrow we push off in one of the biggest attacks of the war. I believe we're ready, and that we'll take our objectives even though we again have the toughest assignment.

What does a soldier think about on the eve of a big job? For me, it's quiet tonight, and I wonder how the guns will be thundering 24 hours from now; I wonder if I'll make it through this job so I can go home. People back home who read of this won't realize how we really live and survive day to day. Are

Dad proudly serves with Col. "Pete" Lynch from training until near war's end. In a 1943 photo, Col. "Pete" (left) and my father (right) engage in a field exercise at Camp Gruber.

the slackers and such enjoying themselves right this minute, as we sweat it out over here? What are all of our loved ones doing right now—are they thinking of us? How I wish this was over so I could be home.

And also I think, please God, let our every move be a successful one, and let me and as many of us as possible see it through. This is what we trained for—I know we're on the right side. God, I hope everything goes well.

Letter from Italy, Thursday, May 11, 1944

Dearest:

Well, I'm shaved, my hair is combed, my stuff is packed to go to the rear, my pistol is clean as a whistle, I've got some K rations, my field glasses, compass, steel helmet, raincoat and field jacket. My morale is okay, I'm scared as hell, I believe everything will be okay, the men are ready and I believe everything is set. . . .

This is really the day and the hour for us, honey. It's the thing every soldier always has way back in his mind from the day he first puts on his uniform. Well, I know. You feel the tenseness, the waiting, and the anxiety in the air. You feel the bigness and the terrific importance of our job. And then you think of the things most dear to you—the real things that count in your life. And then you feel sort of closer to God than ever before—and you pray for success, that our attack will smash the enemy to bits, that maybe this is the final beginning of the end. The time now is in minutes until many of my friends attack in the face of death. In just one minute. I love you. It's on.

Bob

Saturday, May 20, 1944

Don't know many things to write that I can even remember of this attack [Mt. Cianelli]. It's really pursuit of those Jerries now.

Things to remember: The long march from 2030 to 1230. The sniper at night when we were asleep. For some, the only pleasure of war, looting. Those damn hills. How little I sleep and how cold it is in the mountains. So good night and I sure wish we all were home.

Sunday, May 21, 1944

In the damnable mountains again, this time north of Fondi. Our command post is set up in an old building. I'm sitting here late tonight with Louis and Col. Coleman; they're writing letters in this dim light. Bogardus [King J. Bogardus Jr.] rests in bed. Wirth is making coffee. So quiet, perhaps deceptively so. We're still in pursuit. Jerry is still running. I'm about run down, running after him.

Things to remember: The dead Jerries in the tank that the 338th knocked out; the stacks and stacks of ammo that Jerry left; the many prepared positions he had. Cooking dinner near Fondi and being fired upon; how happy the Italians have been to see us at all places; M.Q. Davis killing five Jerries. These damn hills. This damn war.

Monday, May 22, 1944

Tonight we're very close to the beachhead, nearer than anyone else believes. Faced a very tough march today over rougher country than can be imagined.

Things to remember: How we stuck out some five miles with no flank secure; watching the 3rd Battalion fire fight. How erratic the Colonel [Fry] seems at times and how he treated the mules. How hard it is for some people to learn. How much I would enjoy good food again and how I'd like to be home. Great goodness!

Letter from Italy, 12:00 p.m., Sunday, May 28, 1944

Dearest:

Well, I'm alive and that's something in this game. We have had unforgettable experiences in this drive and you can believe our outfit has always had the toughest assignments. Where we've gone no reporter has followed—I'll promise you and I know. Right now I'm watching a little battle across the valley—this is only a small one—the town of Roccagora [possibly Roccagorga] has already fallen to us. Just now an Italian brought us a helmet of wild cherrys [*sic*]. They're good. The local people greet us with flowers, eggs, vino and kisses. Boy, I could stand some of yours, honey.

The roughest terrain, the impassable mountain strongholds, the places where even mules couldn't get in supplies have been ours. For four days planes dropped our food and ammo. D and K rations when we get them are our food. We never sleep. We are dead on our feet but we got the Jerry bastard on the run and we're after him hot and fast. That's a thrill!

. . . I pray this horrible nightmare was over. Boy, we've really got an outfit. I'll write when I can.

Bob

V-mail from Italy, Tuesday, May 30, 1944

Dearest Moms:

Well, while we have a day or so rest before we resume the chase, here's a note. I know you wonder if I've had a part in all this over here. I can assure you I surely have. Our outfit has had the toughest tasks, as time later will reveal, and I've been right smack in the middle. We beat the best he's [the Germans] shown so far and we've got him on the run. Believe me, he's a fighter but soon he will stop. Then will come a test for both sides. The stuff he has abandoned makes us know we have hurt him and that he never dreamed we could move so fast. The memories of this are countless. Believe me, the thrill of victory is great—of being in the underrated Infantry is greater. I'm well. We rest for

Close-up of map on which Dad marks positions of expected troop movements through Rome. As regimental G-3 officer (Operations and Training), he is involved in details of troop movements.

two days and lick our wounds and we're off again. I miss you and love you. Don't worry and tell everyone 'lo for me.

Robert Lee

Friday, June 2, 1944

Today we're in the II Corps Reserve, just east of Valletri [possibly Velletri]. Two motor moves the last two nights; resting now. Went on reconnaissance with Col. Fry and Mac this morning. I was driving. We observed dead Jerries alongside the road, knocked out guns and vehicles. My feet and body are still so sore from all the long marches. How I'd like to be home! New orders and we move again.

Things to remember: Hearing from home and getting the box of sardines and chili, the camp stews we cooked, being mortared near ROCCASECCA, what good eggs Kessle and MQ [M. Q. Davis] and Bill and Schiessler [Lt. Russell F. Schiessler] are. How everybody wishes [Col.] Pete was with us. How I wish that peace would come.

Monday, June 5, 1944

We are past Rome by ten miles tonight, up in the hills again. We fought our way into Rome yesterday. Got in the city about 8 p.m. and then spent until about 5 a.m. getting to bridges over the Tiber [the Tiber River, which flows through Rome to the Tyrrhenian Sea]. I saw nothing of the city itself at all. I think I could have gone back for a look today if Pete were here.

Things to remember: Our command post in Rome's outskirts near the statues, and the shelling of our command post and the bridges, the reception from the people as we moved through the city, eating a can of chili outside Rome and thinking of home.

Thursday, June 8, 1944

Got to MONTEROSA yesterday and last night we were relieved by the 351st. Laid on our can all day too. What a "wonderful" command post. Of all places to select from, we are in an old wreck of a building with a dead mule partly eaten on the bottom floor and three or four dead animals outside. It was Fry's own selection. SNAFU as usual.

Troops take Rome on June 5, 6, and 7. From a packet of photos by the Official War Pictures Co., American troops advance through Rome.

Photo from Official War Pictures Co. depicts members of the 88th raising one of the first flags over Rome.

Letter from outside Rome, Friday, June 9, 1944

Dearest Alice:

For several days now we've been resting here some 20 miles north of the big city. Most of us have had the opportunity to get a little more sleep, including me, and I needed it badly. There's very little I can actually tell you, yet there seems to be so much that I have to say. On the day the city fell, we were fighting our way into the eastern outskirts and then during the hours until about 3:00 a.m. on the 5th we moved with greater ease to two of the bridges over the Tiber. We had a little tough time there. I know definitely Satch's outfit came into the city from the south as we hit it from the east. I'll never forget the enthusiasm of the people as our soldiers passed through, nor the early morning when daylight came as our outfit cleared the edge. We saw almost nothing of the beautiful sights or showplaces. Now with the city relatively safe, all the rear echelon units of service and supply, AMG [Allied Military

Government of Occupied Territories], and administrative branches are in the city. Those Officers and EMs are having a swell time, I'll bet.

When we came through, the people offered us wine, champagne, eggs, threw flowers and confetti at us, and men and women of all ages would hug us and kiss us and shake our hands. Boy, they've got some pretty signorinas there too. People are very well dressed: silk stockings, new clothes and a lot of stuff you apparently can't buy in the States. The town proper is practically unhurt. All this we saw and experienced as we breezed by.

Right now, being only some 20 miles away, we all could go back to see the place and "unlax" a little over a bottle or two of vino or cognac—BUT with this Colonel who took Col. Lynch's place you haven't a chance to unlax a bit. . . .

Had your letters of May 14 and 19 yesterday. I got a kick out of what you say about how the "Allies seem to be doing pretty good in Italy." Hell, honey, I'm no innocent bystander in this push. Our outfit has had the toughest of assignments and have done well. How do you think we got this side of Rome? Have you read anything of our Division yet? It's been released that our Division is in it.

Just had a radio message from an Aggie nearby that he thinks Satch's command post is about three miles up the road. Will ask the Colonel if I can go up. Sure will be good to see the U.S. again and to have this war over with. Hope the invasion continues well, but it will still be a long time, I'm afraid. Don't send baseball news—no time to read such stuff. Send me some sardines. And no more fox hole pillows—they're silly to begin with. Just to fool you all. I love you.

Bob

Excerpt of letter from Italy, Friday, June 9, 1944

Dear Moms:

As you know, the advance over here has been very rapid. There have been times when we actually fell where we stopped, we were so exhausted. We were in the mountains so very much and that going is rough, believe me. For three days we were isolated. In fact, the Jerries were all around us—which isn't the best military tactic—and we were supplied by air. Well, we finally took Rome; our outfit fought its way in from the east which of course there were other units on all sides hitting Rome at the same time. . . . Sure glad the invasion [D-Day] started—this landing possibly isn't the ONE though. I hope they plow right on through. Time to go to bed, Ma. Please tell O'Pa and everyone 'lo and take care of yourself. Don't worry; I'm okay. I love you and miss you.

Robert Lee

Sunday, June 11, 1944

Rainy Sunday morn; sitting and waiting, since we have been ordered to rest and retrain. A few days ago I saw a dead mule, partly eaten, on the bottom floor of an old wreck of a building that the Colonel had chosen for our command post. They say Rome is a paradise: the women are plentiful, beautiful and willing. I could stand a little of that, believe me. Even Varga pictures [Vargas Girls] damn near drive you wild. Some Officers are going to Rome on the side and all the rear boys are there. Everybody is restless at doing nothing—it's even hard to read. We're a little dubious about the invasion progress—beachhead is not very deep. I went to Satch's camp but just missed him. I hope when I see Alice she doesn't have her hair fixed in a knot on her head. I don't much like it in the pictures she sends. What would it be like on a rainy Sunday back home again, to read the paper in bed, to just loaf a little, to see Alice?

Things to remember: Picking up the power generator and battery charger and German radios, what a signal dump. Sally [propagandist Axis Sally, an American employed by the Nazis] says, "The 85th fights like Germans—the 88th like a bunch of cutthroats."

CHAPTER 7

July–September 1944

"How I pray to live from minute to minute; how badly I want to go home."

Letter from Italy, Monday, July 10, 1944

Dearest:

'Tis Monday night, 11:40, and Great Glory, how I wish I were home. Here I sit beside Collier who is talking to some Officer many miles away, judging from how loud he is speaking. Today has been a great day for our Regiment, and for me. I'm alive!!! Boy, you all *can't* know how wonderful that makes you feel. You can never know what those words mean, honey. Our outfit really moved through some tough stuff today, and I suppose this was as rough a day as your husband ever had. Be sure to keep your fingers crossed, honey.

Here are a couple of souvenirs—someday we'll tell our kid that a tin helmet was responsible for him. It's not nice to ask where the German money came from. Just keep these articles for our scrapbook. Must close; I love you so much. Keep your fingers crossed. Mark this day on our calendar.

Bob

[In 2020 I opened this letter for the first time. I found a thin sliver of metal, approximately one and a half inches long. As I read the letter, the shrapnel fragment fell from my hand. My husband and I searched the sofa where I had opened the letter, then the rug, moving furniture as we did so. We could never find it. Perhaps it had fallen into one of Dad's six or so large bins surrounding me. We have searched for it several times over the years. No luck.]

German money is shown still taped to a page in Dad and Alice's scrapbook.

My father saves this invitation to a 350th beach party. It is scheduled for 3:00 on July 2, but he arrives late, around 8:30 pm.

Saturday, July 15, 1944

When I had time, I didn't feel like writing—been long, tho'. I never got a pass to see Rome—screwed there! Did go to SORRENTO. Mike was there from our outfit and so was Griffin. The 350th had a beach party on July 2 when I had to work so I didn't get there until 2030.

Things to remember: The air raid on Civitavecchia; Corbett [Maj. Corbett Williamson] telling Mortimer Snerd off; moving into the line July 5; the attack on the 7th against Volterra, and today how the 88th spearheads the whole front in this damn country, and how we are way out in front. The constant threat of counterattacks and being chopped off, out on a limb. The real honest-to-goodness shellings we've been getting; the machine gunner kicking up dust by my feet; the screaming meemies; the snipers; the good old steel helmet; the shock at Bill Ott's death—and then Benedetto's—at Vick's—at Hennessey's—at Sgt. Parker's, and God knows the others too. How badly I want this to be over, how happy I am to get letters from Alice and Ma. How I can manage to exist without sleep—five out of six nights with almost no sleep, and 25 hours total in six days and nights.

The castle at Cedri as our headquarters, and the big shot Fascist's house at Ghizanno [Ghizzano], the countless paintings, the linen closets, the beautiful furniture, the barrels and barrels of wine.

But to remember above all: The hate, disgust, despair and contempt that some Officers and men have for Col. Fry. How they loathe Col. Cochran's stupidity, how everybody—EVERYBODY—would love to see them both out. How miserable it is for me; how I miss home and Alice; how everybody holds him responsible for practically ordering some men and Officers killed unnecessarily; how the "Social Security Platoon" operates; how near the command post is to the front; "Die with Fry" and how I pray I live from minute to minute; how badly I want to go home.

Letter from Italy, Monday, July 24, 1944

Dearest:

This must be a beautiful morning back home, for even here the sun is bright and the mountain tops are shining above the fog and mist-covered valleys below them. The woods and vineyards and olive trees are such a bright green. Funny, all this beauty of God and still men are dying a few hundred yards away. You know, a man experiences some funny feelings and thoughts in war. I wonder how I'll be and act when I come back. We're in a big castle again on top of a big mountain. Darling, the furniture is beautiful. The table we have all our maps on is tremendous; it must be 50 or 60 feet long with massive, carved legs and a big, heavy top. On the sides of the room are huge cabinets—one has eight doors and on each door is a big carved head of some wild animal, or dog or horse. In other rooms are linen closets, enough to outfit a hotel like the Rice [the well-known Rice Hotel in Houston, Texas] several times over. The linen is beautiful. I'm using towels monogrammed for the duke who lived here. There are closets of lace and curtains and tapestry—the good silver is all gone. There is still some glassware. Here all the huge oil paintings have been destroyed. In another castle we stayed in a short while ago the paintings were intact. We try to keep our boys from plundering and taking too much stuff. They're good about it. . . .

There are quite a few onion and potato patches and also tomato patches in this part. The Officers don't get them often—tomatoes, I love, as you know—so far I had one which my driver brought me when we stopped for a day. Fresh potatoes twice—we boiled them in a tin can and caught hell from Col. Fry for destroying a garden. . . . I sure want to come back, safely and quickly. And I want to find you just as I left you, honey—no changes at all. Take care of yourself and don't work too hard. I love you,

Bob

Letter from Italy, Tuesday, August 8, 1944

Dearest Alice:

BOY, BOY! We Officers each got one bottle of whiskey ten minutes ago. I got a bottle of old Schenleys [bourbon whiskey]—my favorite. Our first ration allowance. I'm hoping that you are laying in a stock of Schenleys—about a dozen bottles for me. Start buying one at a time now. And make it the brand I love or Canadian Club. No other kind! All this you've read about beer over here—we've had beer twice, one bottle per two Officers. The last I had was sort of flat and I had one drink, then let the rest go. Ho hum! I don't mind—all I'm waiting for is for this damn thing to end and get home to you. And all the good things of life back there at home.

Well, supper time. Take care of yourself, honey, and be very sure you get plenty of rest. I love you and miss you very much.

Bob

Friday, August 25, 1944

Again I've been lazy, I guess. Funny, I used to not be. Much. May be the war. We came out of the line on July 29 and moved to St. Vivaldo, stayed there until August 22 and then moved to Leghorn [English name for Livorno] where we've got a [Regiment] gut-Corps Reserve. What a crew is in the line.

Remember since last entry: The constant and steady dislike all have for Fry and the accepted stupidity of Cochran. . . . No use entering all the very ridiculous things, except Mac is out as S-1 and Joe Morey, an old Pointer [West Point], is in.

As I write this I sit in Hotel Excelsior in Rome. I came down on the 22nd and return today. What a place: the bar, the atmosphere, the total relaxation of civilians and soldiers from war. I viewed the Vatican and its wealth too. Unbelievable, the absolutely indescribable Rome atmosphere, the countless beautiful women in this place. Surely no city can rival it.

Friday, September 8, 1944

And now in the 38th Evac [evacuation hospital] since August 30, with sand fly fever; not bad, just one hell of a headache. I remember the nights I couldn't sleep, so nervous and scared—and with trench mouth. Collier came down and Costello—the salt of the earth. . . . We're listening to the good news of the Allies in France, Belgium and Holland. Please, God, make this war end quickly.

What will I do for a living when it's all over? Mostly I dream of seeing sweet Alice again and loving her, never to leave her again. And seeing Moms and Bud and home. Bud is there now. Reading the demobilization plan, it looks like at least six months after peace before we can leave for home. I believe it's Japan for us, though.

Things to remember: The urge you feel back here to be up front helping to finish off the Jerry bastards; the urge you feel up there to be back here where it's safe. Man is funny, or maybe it's just me; probably is.

Remember also: Leaving Rome at 2400 and getting home at 0530, Fry regretting my pass and giving me the problems to prepare that same morning. Everyone is talking about peace—won't that great day ever come?

Remember also: The sincere way the other Officers greeted me in Rome. It's a good feeling to know you're honestly liked by your fellow man.

Letter from near Mt. Battaglia, Monday, September 25, 1944

Dearest honey:

There's not much time now, but I would otherwise try to tell you what a terrific job this push is. Absolutely the fighting could not be more severe anywhere on any front. The resistance is stronger, and the weather and the mountains make this operation indescribable. Jerries are everywhere: in front, on each side and in back, all around. I actually have for the past several

Dad saves two of these souvenir booklets from the Hotel Excelsior. Inside one of them he lists the officers' names, left to right: Col. Davis, Capt. Haegstrom, Capt. Bogardus, Lt. Morrison, himself.

nights slept (?) with a gun in my hand and my steel helmet on my head. You hardly dare show yourself anywhere day or night. It's the worst I've seen.

I remember once your reading me Jack's letter when he said Jap planes flew overhead several times. I sort of shuddered and hoped I never would get that close to the war. Well, yesterday, darling, our Jerry friends put something like 200 or 300 rounds of artillery and mortar fire in here within 150 and much fewer (!!) yards from right here. You get awful close to the good Lord during those times. Food is just another thing—we've eaten twice in two days now, and tomorrow's menu calls for two meals. You just can't get the stuff up here. Your mule pack trains are hunted and shot up by snipers, ambushed at darkness and throughout these dark, rainy and foggy nights. But all of this and the other grim realities sort of make you proud to belong to the best of the lot—the Infantry.

This is not a scare letter; it's no more than you or anyone else knows, who thinks straight. I write it this way so I can remember some of the details when I get home—the details which I want to forget now. So save this letter and show your folks if you care to. This I don't want to talk about right when I get home.

Pray this mess ends soon. Tell Moms you heard from me. I miss you and I love you very dearly.

Bob

Note from near Mt. Battaglia, September 28, 1944

For NCO on duty:

If a Col. calls and wants to talk to Gen. ______ wake him up. If you want the Art. Officer he is right opposite us in a room. Waken Major Melcher in case anything happens. Shake him like hell.

Costello

CHAPTER 8

October–December 1944

"No rest, no sleep, no peace, no appetite."

Letter from near Mt. Battaglia, Friday, October 6, 1944

Dearest honey:

These damnable guns actually shake the earth in our tent, here where we now are. Boy, you have never heard such noise in all your days—thank goodness they are ours going off at the Jerries! I hope each round kills a million. We came out of the lines yesterday. That's why we're back here where the artillery is, resting. "Resting" with these guns going off! As long as they are ours, okay.

This last operation *was* an operation! These damn Jerries are fighting harder than ever. The prisoners are excellent soldiers, with the best and latest equipment. We've been hurt; I doubt if we'll ever be the same. I mean our outfit. The experiences of this one, I'll never forget. They surpass any others I've had. To hell with the people who say Jerry's morale is low. Everybody knows that except Jerry. And everyone knows he's whipped except Jerry. All the prisoners know what's happening in and to their country, too—don't think they don't. It's amazing really, and those darn newspaper articles that mislead the people! Well, the Gothic Line may not be broken for some 30 miles or all along to the Po River, but boy, it's badly cracked and *we're* the boys who hurt the Jerries. We were way the hell out there and *we* were hurting too, when some of our friends finally had to relieve us. But to bring us to this place to "rest" beats me. The artillery fire is incessant, and yesterday Jerry threw some counter-battery in here at us. The night before when some of our first troops arrived, he strafed and bombed this place. So Collier and I enlarged one of the craters by our tent and made us a fox hole. Of course, the hole is full of water and mud is about ten inches deep, but what the hell—we're alive. And some day in two or three years, we'll be home, maybe. Anyhow, we'd lots rather be here in Italy dodging shells every minute, marching day and night soaked to the skin in mud over our ankles, freezing cold, up and down mountains and trails where men and mules disappear over the cliffs, not knowing where you are, just that Jerries are all around you—yeah, we'd much rather do that than be home fussing about some "important" things. Honey, so help me, I've become in such a state of mind that I hate those who dodged the draft . . . I've no use for any of 'em.

Gosh, two pages of this. I'm sorry. Don't mind me; I forgot not to write such stuff. I'm okay. Just wish that on this night I was home with you with the rain beating down on our roof and the wind blowing. By the way, we're due to get a 75 mile-an-hour gale and storm tonight, so I'd better go fasten down my tent a little better. Write, send some pictures, take care of yourself and love me—and keep your fingers crossed. I love you more,

Bob

Friday, October 6, 1944

Sitting here in a tent with Collier, Simpson and Standish, in mud up to our knees. We're going up again tonight. "Our morale is lower than an Italian woman's breasts," quoted Simpson. Well, what an operation.

Fry reached the peak this time—no adequate words. The battle on Battaglia is the greatest for the Regiment so far. Lots to remember on this trip. We started on this trip about three miles southeast of Firenzuola on September 21 and got back here near Valsalva yesterday at noon. The 2nd moved up yesterday evening, the rest of us today.

Things to remember: The rain, fog, mud and mules; getting lost with the Pisano as a guide—too much fog; Col. Bare [Walter E. Bare Jr.], Pitts, Barquist, Romano, Murphy, Ashcraft and McCabe captured in their command post; the message when Collier got it that night; how May jumped out of the window. Moving our command post at night, black as hell, through the woods with firing all around and not really knowing where we were going. Sniper Mt., our command post as a bull's eye with 200 or 300 rounds of mortar and artillery on us. Snipers firing through the door;

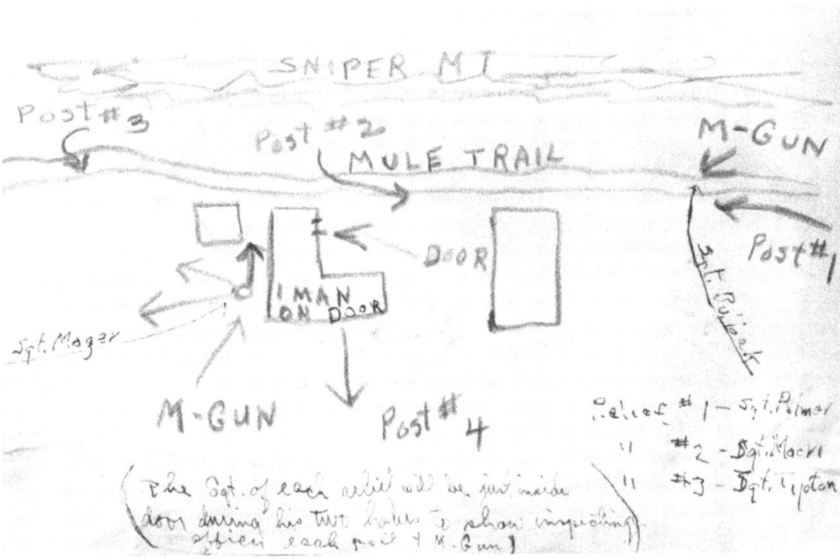

This hand-drawn map of Sniper Mountain [Mt. Battaglia campaign, one of the costliest in terms of dead and wounded troops] states at the bottom, "The Sgt. of each relief will be just inside door during his two hours to show inspecting officer each post and M-gun." Relief sergeants' names are listed, 1–3, Palmer, Macri, Tipton. On movement arrows are named Sgt. Mager and (illegible).

the attack on the house that night and how scared we were. Collier seeing a Jerry in the window; my going to pieces with Col. Fry, sitting on the rock with him waving the map at Mike; becoming a rear echelon man; the many, many wounded and dead.

Collier and me in the dog house, the fight on Battaglia. The mules, mud and rain.

Remember also: The British finally coming to relieve us. The 6th Infantry Battalion helping us on the ridge; the terrific artillery and mortar fire; being shot at again and again by snipers and artillery and being so damn tired of war and K rations. The shortage of rations; the zipper pistols; how we almost moved into the command post where the 1st Battalion staff was captured. Our command post in a church on Valla Maggori [possibly Valle Maggiori]—who says Americans don't take advantage of religious buildings? How the boys looked when they came by our command post as they were relieved on Battaglia; the unbelievable sights of our wounded streaming back to the aid station—things no newsreel can capture.

The wonderful work of Stratman [Edward J. Stratman] and Stoner and all of our surgeons under the most trying conditions and circumstances. The strain and burden on our motors, to say nothing of our men. The 1,014 dead, wounded and missing from September 22 to October 5 and they are still recovering bodies. Costello and Allenbrook telling me about the dirty coffee water . . . afterwards. How we are all starting to talk about rotation and pray that we will be the first. Church services in tents or olive orchards or anywhere and how they comfort you.

Thursday, October 12, 1944

Not near any town, just in the mountains as is usual for us. It's cold tonight but not raining for a change. Our command post is in the basement of an old flour mill right by a river. The flour bins remain half full. We haven't advanced much in the last two days. Jerry is fighting like mad and his artillery, mortars, and SPs [self-propelled guns] are giving our boys hell. One just came in trying for some of our artillery down by the river. My helmet sure makes me feel better. Mike got it today. We were on the staff together so long. God, how we all hope and pray this is over quickly. We are getting quite a few POWs, and it seems strange talking to them [in German]. They will live better now [as our POWs] than ever. Mighty happy that I got letters from Alice and Moms yesterday. Sure would like to be home—goodness.

Also got the *Texas Aggie* [college publication] (remember Maj. Smith class of '31 from Gonzales and the place where I met him). Maj. Cheek, 2nd Battalion, class of 1939 at A&M, is here with us on this job. Yezak is a Senator [Herman Yezak, Texas legislator, 1945–1963] and going home in November. Wish I was.

Letter from Italy, Thursday, October 12, 1944

Dearest Alice:

Had three letters from you and one from Moms yesterday—mighty sweet and made me mighty happy.

Not very nice to say, I guess, but I just found a flea I've been hunting since yesterday. We have them over here like dogs have them in the States. No wonder. I haven't had my clothes off now since September 21. Shoes, yes, at times. This is a pretty mean job, this one. Jerry gets madder, seems like to us. The bastard doesn't know when he is whipped. A lot of the Jerries want to give up, and would, but their Officers would shoot them if they started our way. I interrogate quite a few when our regular interrogator is elsewhere or busy. My German is much better now, and I have very little difficulty G-2-ing [gaining intelligence from] them. No rain today, thank goodness, so the Air Corps boys decided to get even more in the war. We saw a large part of the 1,200 bombers give the Po Valley a workout. Too bad they don't always hit just the Jerries. Maybe we are hard to distinguish from them.

LATER—Business interfered so now to awaken my relief. The hard floor will feel good, for I'm tired. Sure wish this was over and you were in the bedroom waiting. Keep your fingers crossed. I love you.

Bob

Sunday, October 29, 1944

> Well, it's now 4 a.m., still on the graveyard watch, and we are still in the mountains—on Mt. GRANDE. We're just still trying to hang on, no more attack left in us. The 351st took a hell of a beating on VEDRIANO. The Division is really shot now. Constant rain and mud, the mules belly deep with 130 pounds on them. This damn fool relieving Williamson, the best Battalion CO in the whole Army. Gen. Clark pinning on the star and the Officers and men getting nothing . . . and some Germans are walking into our lines and tents, trying to give up.

V-mail from Italy, Saturday, November 4, 1944

Dearest honey:

Right now it's cold, clear and beautiful with all the stars in the world out. Just the sort of night to lie in bed in a warm room, look out of the window and plan on a duck hunt for this weekend. Then turn over, kiss you and snuggle up real close together. Oh my!

Well, we're still in the line—lots of rumors of being relieved but no one believes them much any more. Haven't bathed since the operation started (September 18). Still same old clothes too. I'm just a cake of mud right now. One more week of this and I'll be dirty, don't you think? Someday when this is all over and we've just finished one of your good meals, maybe we can sit back and laugh at some of these experiences. Maybe then, but not now 'cause it isn't so funny. I hear there's a good press release coming out on our outfit when we took Mt. Battaglia. Watch for it. That was a rough one, honey. Take care of yourself. Tell your folks hello. I love you and I miss you.

Bob

Friday, November 17, 1944

We came out of lines on November 7 and moved to MONTECATINI near PISTOIA. I'm now on the last leg of my three-day pass in Rome. Stratman [Capt. Edward J. Stratman] came along in my jeep. Excelsior is very refined this time. I tied on a beauty yesterday—or so I hear. I wrote Bud at Camp Croft [a training camp in South Carolina] today. He still wants to be a hero.

Things to remember: Coming around the corner in that town—lucky me. Simpson falling in the river. The counterattacks on MONTE CALDERARO and Lynch's grand work.

Excerpt, letter from Italy, Tuesday, November 21, 1944

Dearest Moms:

The people in Rome are suffering a lot from lack of food and I'm afraid that a lot of people are going to be cold this winter. But maybe they know not to support dopes like Hitler and Mussolini the next time, if given the choice. . . . The war news in the past few days has been better again; I just hope they can effect a breakthrough at Aachen and Cologne—that's the place to watch, I think. There and north from there. Then too, Russia is due to start something just north of Warsaw. That will be important. Oh well, I just hope Germany gives up the ship. But she feels she is fighting for her existence now. . . .

Robert Lee

Saturday, November 25, 1944

Came back in line on November 19 along a road north of Loiano; our command post is at Cavezzo. We relieved the 338th and we're to hold. This seems like Minturno all over again, except that Col. Pete isn't here. I never was so anxious to go home or get out of an outfit as I am now. I don't know why, but it seems like I'm more nervous now than ever before. I mean really nervous. I guess I pray almost all the time. Work has been unusually heavy, and I almost feel like someone is trying to drive me to quit or give up or something. Damn if I'm not ready, too. Sometimes I don't think I can stand it.

We have a new Major, an ex tanker who has never been in Infantry so they make him Assistant Exec. Louis [Collier] and I continually catch hell, it seems like. Of the two of us, I catch the most. Mentally, this is about to get to me; I've never felt like this before. I sure miss sweet Alice and Moms. How I'd like to be home. I am not doing much sleeping. Every little noise upsets me. There's more work and details to unscrew and put up with than ever before. Louis doesn't seem to worry much, but damn I can hardly stand it. I am even dreaming crazy things the few occasions when I actually do go to sleep. No rest, no sleep, no peace, no appetite.

Awfully miserable.

Sunday, December 3, 1944

I am in 64th General [hospital] now. On the 29th, Dr. Stratman evacuated me, he says for sinus problems, to do something to stop my headaches. Also for my foot that has been infected ever since the fighting at Mt. Grande, first one foot and then the other. I've taken boxes of aspirin, codeine and sleeping pills. The 56th Evacuation Hospital where I had stayed two nights was swell—it was well organized and efficient. This place is different, but I hope I can rest a little. The x-ray done at the 56th shows sinus trouble so that's why I'm here.

Yesterday a year ago I left the States. This past year and the one when Alice was sick shouldn't both happen to any man. Both years were immeasurably long.

The front now is generally quiet; Jerry acts up once in a while and puts all of his artillery on one spot. Jerry sure gave the 133rd hell the other night, with about 600 rounds in 30 minutes. News from France is good again; boy, how I wish this war was over. I'm afraid we will have to go to the Pacific, though, when this is over in Italy. Man, I hope not! I slept good the first two nights and days in the hospital (the 56th). Then I started dreaming again last night. They really examine you here.

Saturday, December 9, 1944

I've been going through one exam after another. A little sinus trouble and headaches but not much. Doc's treating it but may have to cut something out. I talked to a counselor and told him how nervous and worried I've been. I haven't told him that it's Fry who affects me so—I don't like to do that. I've been taking sleeping pills every night and I'm still having wild dreams occasionally. I'll never forget the after-effects of the urology exam. The damn nurse didn't tell me to stay in bed. I've been writing Alice and Moms regularly. They don't know yet that I'm here; no need to worry them.

Dad sends this Christmas greeting to his wife, with no mention of his hospitalization.

Letter from the hospital, Tuesday, December 12, 1944

Dearest Moms:

Well, when you get this, Christmas with all its spirit of thankfulness, prayers, remembrances of those missing, and even its holiday spirit will be past, I'm sure. And for some it *will* be past, but for others I guess there is always a sort of mood of thinking and praying and wishing that tomorrow peace will come. Boy, I'm always hoping that—always that tomorrow will see peace.

If I had told you before, I'd know you would have worried even tho' there is absolutely no need to. So I waited until Christmas was over—I know you've had plenty to do. The same goes for Alice and I'm telling her tonight too. Since November 29 I've been in a hospital. The reasons: I had an infected foot for about three weeks and had to get off it; I was getting sort of nervous because I wasn't getting enough sleep and because things weren't going right—so the doctor just called me one day and the next thing I knew he evacuated me to a hospital. I've had and am still having every kind of complete physical exam they can give. I'm happy to tell you that with a very few exceptions I'm physically pretty good. . . . So there you have the story. It's absolutely nothing to worry about. They're giving me some medicine, I still have some tests to take, and they are making me sleep a lot.

My outfit is still in a quiet sector; there's nothing much happening up there. So this was a good time for me to get straight. . . . Ma, again—you can see it's no need to worry. Tell O'Pa and everyone 'lo. Also Bud and Helen when you write them. Take care of yourself. I love you.

Robert Lee

Excerpt, letter from Italy, Wednesday, December 27, 1944

Dearest Moms:

I can't begin to tell you how very, very sorry I was to hear of O'Pa's [his maternal grandfather's] death. I loved the old man so much and looked forward so to sitting and listening to him talk of old times again. I really respected him for what he accomplished in his 88 years and for his wisdom. He knew and learned a lot. I'm so glad he died peacefully. Be sure to let Mannie and Tante [Aunt] Puttle and Tante Lieschen know how I feel.

You know, Ma, I can remember so well when I was a little kid how he used to "ride" me on his tremendous foot and leg. I hope when I'm 88 that I can look back over as full a life as he had. . . .

Robert Lee

CHAPTER 9

January–April 1945

"How very dear life can be when death is so close."

Sunday, January 7, 1945

So I start a new year still over in this country. Well, God was good to me and I'm living, which some of my friends can't say . . . Mike, Skalby, Hennessey, Vick, Ott, Walter E. Bare, Pitts, Borquist, Romano, Benedetto, and goodness knows how many junior Officers and enlisted men. Who will take their places at home? And we are a civilized people! Yet right now shells are going off that kill men who so desperately want to live. But you can't think of that in a war. I have difficulty still in trying to sleep, thinking of what tortures, mental and physical, those fellows up on the front have to go through, the hell of having to watch always for your very life, in all kinds of weather, the feeling you get that the next artillery shell or the next mortar round is coming right at you, how very dear life can be when death is so close, how very scared you are for yourself—and for those you know so well, too.

Will you see them again when they leave? If people only knew the truth at times about the war.

Better feelings: The rumor yesterday that I was to be Z.I.'d [assigned to the Zone of Interior]. May God see me through this year as He's been with me in 1944—and may He bring an early peace to this world so the terrible tragedy of war will cease forever. [This is] my constant prayer—and for the safekeeping of Alice, Moms, Bud, Helen and all of our loved ones.

Things to remember in the hospital: Waiting for the mail from Alice and Moms, only four letters from her and two from Moms since November 27; packages from Moms, Alice, Bud, Leon and Gladys [a cousin and his wife], the Blekers [Alice's parents] and the Bonnens. Also the lovely picture from Alice and how much it makes me love her, the letter from Bubs Davis, being visited by Bubs, Coles, Haegstrom [Floyd A. Haegstrom], Laramie, Curley, Sanford, Hulbert, Taylor, Fingerhut [Capt. Walter C. Fingerhut], Sgt. Sallee, Aimee, and their sincere expressions, also the letters from Louis, the S-1 and Headquarters Co. boys, Costello, Allenbrook. They made me feel as if I used to mean something to the Regiment. Also, Christmas in the hospital and how the nurses worked so hard fixing up the wards.

Excerpt, letter from Italy, Sunday, January 14, 1945

Dearest Moms:

I've gotten several more of your and Alice's letters. One of hers was very nice and sounded like her. Also a box from her of two mufflers to slip over your head—why two? And another pair of gloves, which I did need. That makes three pair she sent this Christmas and a pair of garters. We wear boots all the time now but I guess she didn't know. Also she sent me a five-foot Christmas tree cut in sections to be put together by pegs. Or did I tell you?

Glad to have your frank opinion about how Alice is. She never says how she feels, and I didn't know for a long time that she had stopped working. Is she having worse headaches? I have written to her dad to see how she is doing. No answer so far. She is such a sweet girl, doing so much for others, I wish she would take more care of herself and rest. . . .

Please remember to pet my dog Spot for me. I love you.

Robert Lee

Letter from Italy, Monday, February 12, 1945

Dearest Moms:

Since I'm assigned to this new job I feel like I haven't done one honest day's work, compared to the way I have worked the other 35 months I've been in the Army. In my way of thinking, they could probably do with about ⅓ as many Officers back here as they have, but so far I'm keeping my big mouth shut and not saying anything.

It's been very wet and darn cold here. But considering everything, it "ain't nothing" in the way of misery, strain, cold and discomfort like it was in the front lines. And I'm extremely thankful for that. If those Jerries would just quit so this terrible world tragedy would come to an end. I do hope the people will do some sound and constructive thinking when the peace is written this time. I am afraid, though, that there hasn't been enough physical hurt to the U.S. to stop all the small quarrels. Take care of yourself. Pet Spot for me. Love,

Robert Lee

Monday, February 26, 1945

Here I am, way back in the G-3 section of Rep'l Com'd [Headquarters Replacement Command]. I thought I was through with "3" work. I resolve to take this job easier; never again like I worked in the 350th! In my interview with the CG [commanding general] on February 4, I asked to be given a job where I would *feel* necessary back here if I was assigned. So after about three days of loafing in Touristico [Turistico] Hotel at Naples, I am here. It's regular hours, an Officers' mess, silverware, multi rank and brass. I'm the only one in "3" section with combat experience, and here they are, training boys in the last stop before the front! This "ain't" no place for me. I miss my buddies in the 350th.

Things to remember: The good letters from the boys: Costello, good old Chaplain Pressly, Smalledge, and Hotch [Thomas A. Hotchkiss]. Also, seven poker games and one crap game so far here, won 6 times, now up $200. The good feeling of having paid my debts, no fleas or lice back here, no shells either, watching the war news, come on Uncle Joe [Joseph Stalin]! Had headaches the first six days, still on a diet of sleeping pills and aspirin. Feeling better, though, thank goodness!

And to remember of my days with the 350th: How the tanks would chew up our telephone lines, the booby traps at the castle at Cedri (where the command post was in front of the line), what a situation! Brison getting killed in the 349th, what an experience this whole war is to me, and always how good it'll be to get back home.

Letter from Italy, Saturday, March 3, 1945

Dearest Moms:

Yesterday I got two boxes from you—the sausage, cheese, pecans, sardines, olives, crackers, canned shrimp, etc. The sausage and everything is

Dad's brother Max ["Bud"] sends him a photo, looking fierce, from somewhere in the Middle East, undated.

delicious. I love you for sending all that stuff. Also I got your letter of February 3 with the enclosed one from Helen. Thank my sister-in-law kindly as I think it was very sweet.

So Bud's transfer didn't go through. Well, he wanted in the Infantry so I guess now he'll get his feet wet.

Ain't no use worrying 'cause he'll be alright, and a much smarter and wiser man when it's all over. I know the house was in a turmoil while he and Vic and their wives were home. Yes, goodness, I'd like to have been there with Alice. I had Uncle Lee's letter yesterday too, and I was very glad to hear from him and Tante Puttle. I hope they are all okay. I'll try to write them this week.

I'm tired, Ma, and there's no more news now so I'll close. Give Alice all my love. Love and kisses.

Robert Lee

Letter from Italy, Sunday, April 15, 1945

Dearest Moms:

I've had the headaches again for the past week or so, but okay now. Also I've been pretty busy lately. I'm glad. Saw several of my old friends from our old Regiment lately. We reminisced but I can't describe the feeling between us. One of our old Battalion commanders now lives near our place. He and I are very good friends. You've no idea how a fellow can miss the other Officers he soldiered with. I miss my old outfit.

All of us were so grieved and shocked at our President's [Roosevelt's] death. Soldiers looked to him as the one who would help fight their battles—a sort of champion. Today we had memorial services for him. I hope people back home find the courage and determination to carry out his ideals.

The war news is very good, of course. I still believe the summer will end and the European War will too. Also watch how much more important the Italian campaign will become.

How are Bud and Helen? Give them my love. Have they received my letters? Tell me everything about them, as I want to know. I mean that! Each one is lucky in having the other. And I also mean that.

Guess the La Grange countryside is beautiful now. I'll bet this is fishing weather back home. My, am I hungry for barbecue. Ma, you could even fry some chicken, put it in Mason glass jars, seal it airtight and I'd have it in three weeks. Boy, I'd sure love some. It's been almost 16 months since I've had fried chicken. Wish I could be there with all of you. Is my old dog Spot okay? Are all his teeth gone now? What do you feed him, Ma? Do you think he'll know me when I do get home? I still laugh when I think of him. Are those pretty red roses of yours in bloom? I surely liked your Easter card and the picture. It was very good and you look like the same Moms to me. I hope you're taking care of yourself. Boy, am I looking forward to coming home and someday putting my feet under the table with you and Alice, Bud and Helen and eating some of your good food. Then to relax and for about a month worry about nothing in the world. I sure miss you and Alice and Bud and Helen and home. The day is much nearer now. I am lucky and thankful. Must close. Write when you can. Love,

Robert Lee

CHAPTER 10

May–August 1945

"I'm praying we're smart enough as a people to never have a war again. I'll do my part."

Letter from Italy, Thursday, May 3, 1945

Dearest Moms:

Today we learned of Italy and part of Austria being surrendered. So part of the long, hard job we started has been completed. We are all a little proud of our part. I hope and pray it'll all be over soon and that hereafter we'll never again have to resort to war to solve our problems. I'm sure the pictures and stories of German prison camps are convincing as to the true nature of Germans. And convincing as to what the U.S. would have been in for, had we not fought when we did. My idea of a German is lots different than what it was. Some of my friends were in those prison camps.

Well, no more news, Ma. We are pretty busy. Take care of yourself. Love,

Robert Lee

Letter from La Grange, Texas, Tuesday, May 8, 1945

My dear boy,

Today my heart is filled with gratitude and thanksgiving to God, for the victory and the end of hostilities in Europe. Since the first of May the news was expected almost at any time, and we knew it was coming, so this morning when our President proclaimed it to our nation, it was almost too good to be true. The wonderful news, for which we have been waiting so long, had

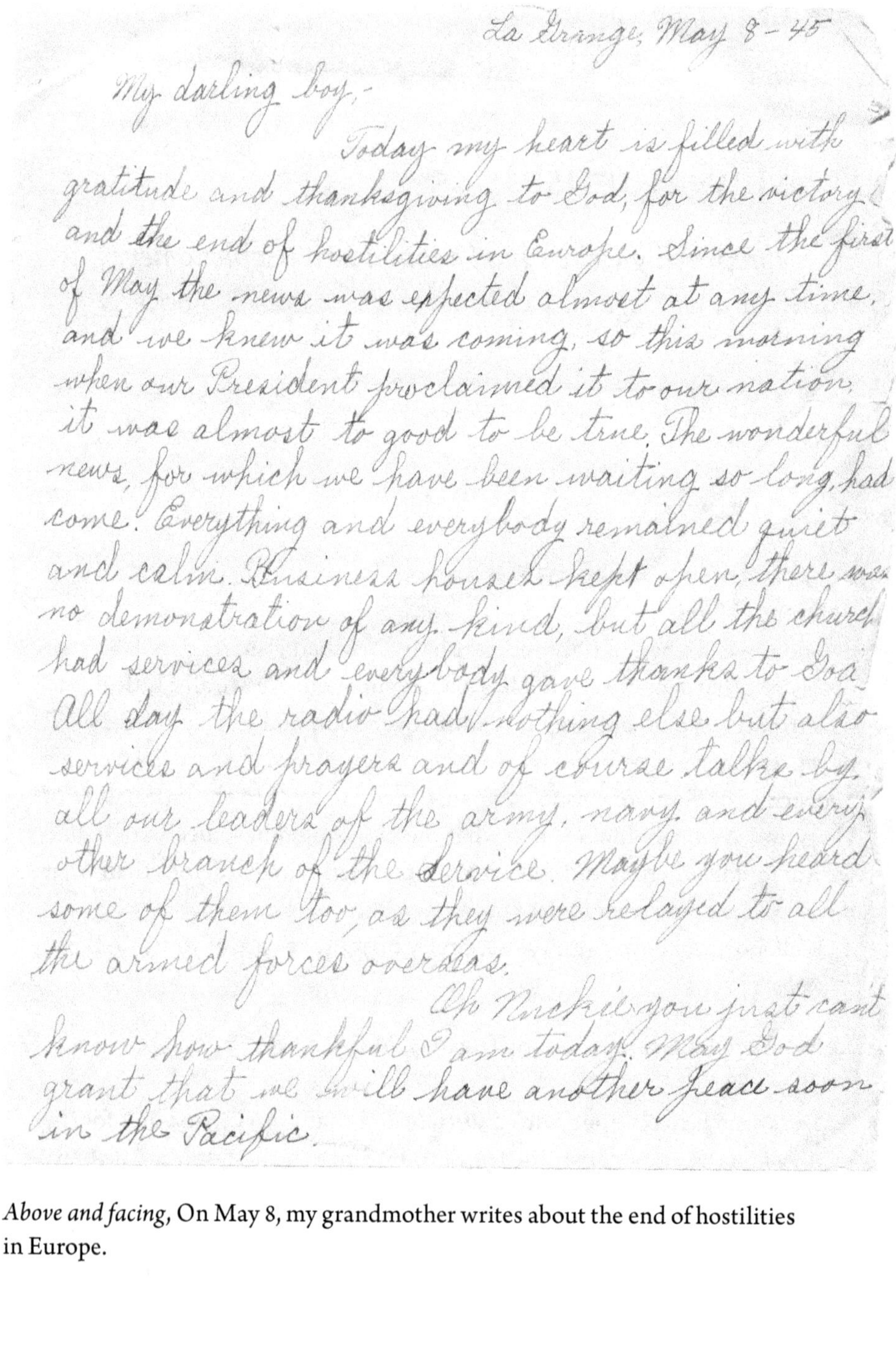

La Grange, May 8 - 45

My darling boy,-

Today my heart is filled with gratitude and thanksgiving to God, for the victory and the end of hostilities in Europe. Since the first of May the news was expected almost at any time, and we knew it was coming, so this morning when our President proclaimed it to our nation, it was almost to good to be true. The wonderful news, for which we have been waiting so long, had come. Everything and everybody remained quiet and calm. Business houses kept open, there was no demonstration of any kind, but all the church had services and everybody gave thanks to God. All day the radio had nothing else but also services and prayers and of course talks by all our leaders of the army, navy and every other branch of the service. Maybe you heard some of them too, as they were relayed to all the armed forces overseas.

Oh Nickie you just can't know how thankful I am today. May God grant that we will have another peace soon in the Pacific.

Above and facing, On May 8, my grandmother writes about the end of hostilities in Europe.

I am wondering how long it will be before some of you boys will be sent home. Maybe you can tell me in your next letter.

I had your letter of the 26th a few days ago, and as always so happy to hear from you. Alice called me last Friday and said she is coming this weekend for Mothers Day instead of last Sunday. I sure will be glad to see her. Nuckie, next to you and Max A. I love her very much.

Max A. came back from Dallas, and while there, a major told him that they needed a man in San Antonio, so he was assigned with the Intelligence there. Isnt that lucky? I am so happy about it. He said he knew he would like his job very much. He said to tell you not to give up looking for his letter, it would get there some day.

Old Spot is happy in his new sleeping quarters. He is sleeping in my new wash house. Everybody is well and so many of our friends send their best to you.

Take care of yourself my dear boy and write. All my love and prayers are with you always.

Your loving Mother.

come. Everything and everybody remained quiet and calm. Business houses kept open, there was no demonstration of any kind, but all of the churches had services and everybody gave thanks to God. All day the radio had nothing else but also services and prayers and of course talks by all of our leaders of the Army, Navy and every other branch of the Service. Maybe you heard some of them too, as they were relayed to all the armed forces overseas. Oh, you just can't know how thankful I am today. May God grant that we will have another peace soon in the Pacific.

I got your letter a few days ago, and as always so happy to hear from you. Alice called me last Friday and said she is coming this weekend for Mother's Day instead of last Sunday. I sure will be glad to see her. Next to you and Max A. [Max Allen], I love her very much. Max A. came back from Dallas, and while there, a Major told him that they needed a man in San Antonio, so he was assigned with the Intelligence there. Isn't that lucky? I am so happy about it. He said he knew he would like his job very much. He said to tell you not to give up looking for his letter, it would get there some day.

Old Spot is happy in his new sleeping quarters. He is sleeping in my new wash house. Everybody is well, and so many of our friends send their best to you. Take care of yourself, my dear boy, and write. All my love and prayers are with you always. Your loving . . .

Mother

Wednesday, May 9, 1945—the Great Day!

> And so it's come at last. Our work in Europe is done. Finished. And the peace we all prayed so earnestly for, so hard and continually for, is here. At 0001 today [one minute after midnight on May 8, the official day of Germany's surrender to the Allies, now celebrated as V-E Day, Victory in Europe Day]. We had been expecting it; all the Jerries in Italy gave up on May 2.
>
> A great blow came right at the last—Charley Lynch [Charles P. Lynch Jr., son of Col. "Pete" Lynch] was killed at the end. I heard that from Harris and Councilman. I have one regret: I'd like to have been with the outfit on the last push. But I'm lucky, I guess. I thank God for seeing me through this war over here; I hope I can show my thankfulness by being a better man.
>
> Over to Rome only four times since March 20 when we moved. I wonder when I'll get home? Will I go to the Pacific? What kind of job waits for me

after it's all, all over? How easy this job is compared to how I used to work. How everyone does just about nothing now.

Feeling better, only a little spell of insomnia for about a week recently, about the time of the push in Italy.

Things to remember: Going back by Roccagorga and Castelforte. How I missed Mike and Skalby and Ott and all the others, especially today. Truly, may they not have given their lives in vain. Councilman telling me that even now not an hour goes by someone doesn't mention my name at the outfit. I'm proud, for I love 'em. And Majors giving parties for Generals and staffs.

I remember from way back: Romano and his mortars, the hit on the man on the stretcher. Also, seeing Col. Walter E. Bare after he escaped from the Jerries, and Fritz Mueller, A&M class of '32, who saw Alice.

I'm praying we're smart enough as a people to never have a war again. I'll do my part.

Wednesday, June 20, 1945

I have been down here in Sorrento since June 13. I'll be leaving on June 21, down via truck with the 1st Depot boys. I am sticking with a doc and a Captain who are very nice. We're just drinking, swimming, relaxing and watching some of the others wolf the nurses. I miss Alice more than ever before in my life. We went to Capri several days ago. It was a let down, but the drive to Amalfi and Revalla [Ravello] was lovely. Met Gleisman, 760th Tank Battalion. The C.O. [commanding officer] said, "Major Melcher was the only man in the 88th we could talk to."

Costello's letter said Scotty and Astin as well as Lynch were killed. What a terrible, terrible pity! Have come by Minturno, Castelforte, Rocassecca [Roccasecca] several times on my trips. Some of the men are writing themselves up for a medal at Headquarters—I never knew how some people could be so exaggerated. I miss sweet Alice more than I ever have before in all my life. I know she is the best in the world.

Letter from La Grange, Texas, Wednesday, July 4, 1945

My dear sweet boy,

I am wondering what you are doing on this 4th of July. I hope that you are well and feeling fine. Here is how I passed the day. Got up at 9:15, by 11 I had eaten breakfast, washed dishes, and read the Post [the *Houston Post* newspaper]. For breakfast I had hot cornbread, bacon, molasses, and coffee.

I was lucky in getting one pound of sliced bacon yesterday, the first since March. I had my name on the list for bacon since then at the grocers. It cost 38 cents a pound and 8 red points, so I didn't buy any meat to save points. You know I get only 50 red points a month, and a pound of butter is 12 points alone, so you see how I have to figure to come out. Nearly every weekend I buy a chicken, which are point free, and once or twice a week I eat supper in town, but meat is served very sparingly. Occassionally [*sic*] one or other of our markets is closed for a week or a few days, whenever they have sold their quota. Still no black pepper to be had, and no toilet tissue and I am on my last roll. Son, the people are really having to learn, to do without things, as far as I am concerned I can get along alright. Eggs sell at 35 cents and milk 13 cents a quart. There is plenty of both to be had. But sugar is very scarce, most large cities are completely out of sugar.

I had your swell letter of June 24, and injoyed [*sic*] it very much. I hope you will get to stay where you are, as long as you have to stay in the Army, and when you leave there, that you will get your discharge and come home to stay. . . .

Take care of yourself my dear boy. All my love and kisses, your loving . . .
Mother

Sunday, July 8, 1945

Boy, I wondered if I'd ever see this day. At 1800 we left Napoli in the *Mt. Vernon*, a swell ship. I'm so thankful and happy to have lived through this and to be going home. My heart is full. Maybe before the end of this month I'll see Alice—and home.

Overseas 19 months and 8 days. . . . So happy to be going home. So happy! I look back on this now and think of the many good, brave men we left behind—and why do we have to have wars? Why should men like Mike, Bill, Skalby, Watson, Charley and so many more have to stay here, dead and buried? Is the world any better because they died?

I hope all my life I can keep them in mind so I'll always fight for honesty and courage and decency—or else I'll feel I'm not doing right by them.

Somehow it doesn't seem right I'm going home to Alice and my folks when they can't go back to their loved ones. This life we live is so confusing.

An undated early photo of the American Cemetery in Florence is sent by a serviceman to Dad. The cemetery eventually encompasses 70 acres, with headstones of 4,392 American soldiers, most fallen after Rome's capture in June 1944, as well as in fighting in the Apennine Mountains.

Wednesday, July 18, 1945

Yesterday, at 1715, I saw land—the good old U.S. And this morn at 0805 we got off the ship at Camp Patrick Henry [in Virginia]. The Red Cross greeted us with doughnuts and ice cold milk. What a sight: These lawns, beautiful green, and white wooden homes! Everything okay and nothing shot up. No dirty kids begging cigarettes or chocolate or pimping. And the pretty American girls! Our first meal here: steak, fresh tomatoes, potatoes and milk and ice cream. What a blessing to be an American.

Wednesday, July 25, 1945

I called Alice twice. It was really swell to hear her voice. The time passes so slowly now but tomorrow we leave. I will go to Fort Sam [Fort Sam Houston, San Antonio, Texas]. Should get there Sunday night so maybe Tuesday I'll see Alice. And then Moms and Bud and home. Maybe the excitement has brought on my restlessness, but I'm still having hell sleeping and dreaming. It'll all be over when I get home though. I hope.

Sunday, July 29, 1945

I got into Fort Sam late in the night and today, about 9:30 p.m., I saw Alice!

Thursday, August 2, 1945

Home in La Grange! And a 30 days leave.

Friday, August 31, 1945

Another 30 days leave.

Monday, October 1, 1945

Back at Fort Sam.

My father's dog tags return with him to the States. Both tags are always worn as part of a soldier's uniform. One dog tag is removed for identification when a soldier is found gravely wounded or deceased.

CHAPTER 11

Significant Events

Recorded in the Closing Pages of my Father's Diary

★ SERVICE RECORD ★

TRANSFERS AND CHANGES IN RANK

6-11-42	ASGD. 88TH DIV.
6-19-42	ASGD. CO. K, EXEC.
7- -42	" S-3, 3RD BN.
10-8-42	PROMOTED TO CAPT
1-28-43	ASGD. S-3, REGT.
6-26-43	PROMOTED TO MAJOR
1-24-45	CLASS "B" DUTY.
2-9-45	ASGD. G-3 SECT., HQS. REPL. COMMAND.
7-8-45	GOING HOME!!

In this section of his diary, Dad records his transfers and changes in rank, 1942–1945.

Editors of my father's war diary, *My Life in the Service*, included a section for soldiers to write down important dates and impressions of places and events they wanted to remember. Below is what my father recorded of his service record, travels, and battles. Just as in the context of his diary, I have confirmed the battles and locations through diligent research (refer to the citations at book's end). I hope that military researchers and students of history can find Dad's first-person timeline useful in adding to or confirming their knowledge of the time.

SERVICE RECORD

PLACES I HAVE BEEN

- Left Houston, 3–11–42 at 5:45 p.m.
- Arrived Fort Benning, Georgia, 3–14–42 at 4:00 p.m.
- Reported at Camp Gruber, Oklahoma, 6–19–42.
- Left Camp Gruber for Louisiana Maneuver Area, 6–13–43.
- Arrived Fort Sam Houston, Texas, 8–28–43.
- Left Fort Sam Houston, 11–20–43.
- Arrived Camp Patrick Henry, 11–23–43.
- Left Camp Patrick Henry, 12–2–43, on ship at 1302 EWT [time zone].
- On African soil at Oran, 12–23–43, at 2050 AWT; actually debarked at 0930 on 12–24–43.
- Left Africa, 12–27–43, at 1415 AWT.
- Landed at Naples, Italy, 1–2–44, at 1007.
- Left for front, 1–3–44, at 0810; first air raid at 1515.
- At Command Post near St. Pietro, 1–6–44 (168th Infantry).
- With the British at Mondragone, 1–12 to 1–23.
- At Tufa on 1–24–44.
- Left the British, 1–26–44, and on to Piedmont.
- To Naples with Mike on 2–2–44; back to Piedmont on 2–23–44.
- 350th moves into line on 3–4–44, then out of line on 3–30–44.
- 350th moves back into line on 4–21–44.
- We move out 5–11–44 with the key point of the whole 5th Army as our objective.
- At Rome 6–4–44, still attacking.

- Two miles south of Monterosa, about 20 miles north of Rome, on 6–7–44; first rest since attack started on 5–11.
- Into the line again on 7–5–44, some five miles south of Volterra; hope I live.
- We've reached the Arno on 7–22–44.
- IV Corps Reserve in vicinity of Leghorn on 8–22–44.
- At assembly area south of Florence on around 9–7–44.
- Back into the line south of Firenzuola on 9–21–44; back out of the line around 10–5–44.
- Back in the line on 10–9–44 north of Castel Del Rio.
- On 11–7–44, back out of the line and to Montecatini.
- To Rome on a three-day pass on 11–14–44.
- On 11–19–44, back in the line west of Highway 65; Command Post at Savazza; M. Fano in sector.
- To hospital on 11–29–44; the 56th for two days and then to the 64th in vicinity of Leghorn.
- On 1–26–45, no more front line for me; on to the 8th Reppo [Personnel Replacement Depot]; vicinity of Florence.
- On 1–31–45, on to the 7th via boat from Leghorn.
- On 2–2–45, at the 7th; vicinity of Napoli.
- On 2–9–45, at Headquarters Replacement Command; vicinity of Caserta; G-3—thought I was through with that "3" work.
- On 7–8–45, leaving Naples on the *Mt Vernon* at 1800. Headed for the U.S.!!
- On 7–17–45, saw land at 1715—the good old U.S.
- On 7–18–45, got off the ship at 0815. What a grand feeling; 19 months plus days overseas; I'm at Camp Patrick Henry.
- On 7–26–45, leaving here for Texas and home!

MY DISCHARGE FROM THE SERVICE

Date: November 2, 1945
Place: Fort Sam Houston
Rank: Major
Comment: Terminal leave runs to February 18, 1946

CHAPTER 12

Inspiration from the Pages

Thoughts to Live By, from the Pages of My Life in the Service

Quotes to inspire the troops were printed at the bottoms of pages throughout editions of *My Life in the Service,* my father's 1941 edition included. Some of these may seem poignant or outdated in today's world, although many of the principles that were expressed then remain applicable today. Many are still relevant, and some may actually apply even more now than they did in the 1940s. Following are selected quotes, as well as some of my father's own words, as indicated by his initials, RLM. All of these—including my dad's words—can be found in the pages of his own war diary.

"The world was never more unsafe for democracy than it is today."
—*Stanley Baldwin*

"Things to remember: To always be kind and considerate of my fellow man. And to never lose my love for the simple, sweet things of life."
—*RLM*

"To God, thy country, and thy friend be true."
—*Henry Vaughan*

"Do your duty in all things. You cannot do more. You should never wish to do less."
—*Robert E. Lee*

"The greater the difficulty, the greater the glory."
—*Cicero*

"The only good thing war brings is the wonderful dream of peace and happiness, and being with the one you love."
—*RLM*

"Worth, courage, honor, these indeed your sustenance and birthright are."
—*E. C. Stedman*

"Confidence begets confidence."
—*Proverb*

"The less there is of fear, the less there is of danger."
—*Livy*

"I hope all my life I can keep them [the fallen soldiers] in mind so I'll always fight for honesty and courage and decency—or else I'll feel I'm not doing right by them."
—*RLM*

"Just draw on your grit; it's so easy to quit—It's the keeping your chin up that's hard."
—*Robert W. Service*

"This is what we trained for—I know we're on the right side."
—*RLM*

"Proclaim liberty throughout all the land unto all the inhabitants thereof."
—*Inscription on the Liberty Bell*

"When we assumed the soldier, we did not lay aside the citizen."
—*George Washington*

"Americanism consists in utterly believing in the principles of America."
—*Woodrow Wilson*

"Independence now and Independence forever!"
—*Daniel Webster*

"What a blessing to be an American."
—*RLM*

CHAPTER 13

Rank, Chocolate, and FUBAR

Echelon, Sustenance, and Slang on the Battlefield

STAFF SECTION DESIGNATIONS

Throughout my father's diary and letters, certain designations were mentioned in reference to fellow officers. These letters and numbers were assigned to staff sections according to their function and responsibility. "S" indicated echelons such as battalions and brigades. "G" referred to levels above. The numbers following each letter did not reflect hierarchy but rather the function within the staff section.

S-1 and G-1 (Personnel)
S-2 and G-2 (Intelligence)
S-3 and G-3 (Planning, Operations, and Training)
S-4 and G-4 (Logistics)
S-5 and G-5 (Civil-Military Operations)
S-6 and G-6 (Signal Operations)

My father spent most of his service in S-3 and G-3.

FOOD IN THE SERVICE

Increasing troop mobility in World War II created a need for lightweight rations of food and supplements that were easy to carry during battlefield or tactical situations. The resulting D, K, and C rations that the US Army issued to its troops were modified and improved throughout the war years. Such improvements were necessitated by changing food shortages, speed of production, better packaging, the ability to ship overseas, and so on.

D rations

D rations were meant to be used as emergency rations for survival. They were produced in great quantities and just slightly improved as the war progressed. Ingredients included dry milk, sugar, raw flour, chocolate, and flavoring to produce a 400- to 600-calorie bar. The bar tasted bitter and was rock hard, and it was meant to be eaten slowly. Soldiers who consumed this bar quickly suffered stomach issues, and for that reason the bar was nicknamed "Hitler's Secret Weapon."

K rations

Light in weight and issued one per day, per soldier, K rations were small, portable packages of three basic meals: breakfast, lunch, and supper. Developed in 1941, K rations were originally intended to be used for emergency sustenance, such as when the supply chain had broken down, the field kitchen had not yet been set up (or could not be, because of situations on the ground), or food could not be obtained from local sources. Although meant to be used only two or three days at a time, K rations eventually became the day-to-day food for most soldiers and were used throughout the war.

K rations could give soldiers' stomachs a full feeling, but they were not appealing to the appetite. According to soldiers, the K rations left them feeling less than satisfied. The typical contents of a day's K ration generally included canned meat such as chopped ham or ham paste, crackers or biscuits, dried fruit, cereal, canned cheese, and water purification tablets. Chocolate, cigarettes, gum, bouillon, sugar, salt, powdered drinks, and even toilet paper added some variety or usefulness. The meals commonly provided approximately 79 grams of protein and 2,830 calories. Soldiers often criticized these rations as bland and monotonous, and providing fewer calories than they needed.

C rations

At times, soldiers' rations were supplemented with C rations. A bit heavier to carry, these canned or tinned "wet" foodstuffs included hash, stew, or meat and were intended to add more flavor and appeal to the soldiers' diet. Unfortunately, just as with the D and K rations, overuse and monotony elicited complaints from the troops.

When possible, troops supplemented their monotonous diets with foods from local sources. These sources included local gardens and shops as well as fruits and vegetables growing in the wild when they could be found. My father wrote of grateful Italians giving troops champagne and food.

SOLDIERS' WISH LISTS

From time to time, hungry soldiers included wish lists in the letters they sent home. Along with their other wishes, such as new socks and warm mufflers or head scarves, they also asked for their favorite—and often spicier—foods. While my father was in Italy, his letters frequently included requests for canned sardines, deviled ham and sausages, saltine crackers, canned chili, and sauerkraut. To spice up his allotted rations, he asked for Lea & Perrins Worcestershire sauce, hot sauce, his mother's homemade preserves, dill pickles, and catsup. Cigars, pecans, and even fried chicken rounded out the requests he sent home to his loved ones, especially his mother. In one letter to "Moms," my dad made sure to instruct her on how to send the fried chicken so it would not spoil.

I have found myself wondering if Dad's typically precise requests were viewed back home as commands. Growing up years later, I experienced quite a few of Dad's commands, and I knew that I had to "finish what I start."

SLANG IN WORLD WAR II

During World War II, with so many Americans serving on the battlefield—often living in close quarters as well—it became inevitable that specialized wording would be created. In some cases, certain terms experienced a rebirth from usage in previous wars. Soldiers used informal language, or slang, in daily conversations with their buddies, and such slang often appeared in the letters they sent home. Occasionally wartime slang turned up in battlefield diaries as well as newspaper and magazine articles of the day. Some phrases used in the 1940s have become obsolete; some can be heard today in daily American conversation. Regardless, such slang can be colorful or entertaining, to say the least.

My father was a grand storyteller all of his life, and he used colorful language at times. He seldom cursed, though, except when telling a joke or two at whiskey-inspired parties after A&M football games (win or lose). I noticed that while he used some slang in his writing, he used only wording befitting an officer when writing in his personal diary.

Military slang of the day included the following words and phrases, some of which appear in Dad's war diary.

Ack ack—antiaircraft fire

Ammo—ammunition

Armed to the teeth—well equipped and ready

AWOL—absent without leave

Baptism by fire—the occasion when a soldier comes under enemy fire for the first time

Batman—an orderly; a soldier or airman assigned as a personal assistant to an officer

Beat your gums—talk too much

Bedpan commando—a medical corpsman

Bit the dust—severely wounded or, more commonly, killed

Blanket drills—taking naps

Bone up on—learn more about; study

Brownnoser/bootlicker—a yes-man, someone who seeks the approval of higher-ups

Bully beef—common British term for canned beef or corned beef

Chicken shit—Army regulations and chores that soldiers did not want to adhere to or perform

Civvies—civilian clothing

CO—commanding officer

Cool as a cucumber—calm and collected

Dear John—a letter in which a soldier's girlfriend breaks up with him

Dog tags—metal identification tags worn around a soldier's neck, two at a time, so that one tag could be removed for identification of a dead soldier and the other could be left with the body

Do one's bit—serve or work in wartime effort in time of war

Eager beaver—a soldier who volunteers for everything so as to impress the higher-ups

Echelon—a subdivision of headquarters; a level of command

Evac—evacuation

File 13—trash basket or trash can

Flak—antiaircraft fire, possibly from German *Fliegerabwehrkanone* (antiaircraft gun)

For the birds—useless or senseless information

Fox hole pillow—pillows sold to loved ones at home, to send to soldiers in battle areas

FUBAR—fouled up or f___ed up beyond all recognition

Get cracking—get started immediately on a task

GI or GI Joe—an enlisted soldier; government issue

Gibson Girls—beautiful poster or pinup models, named after the artist Charles Gibson

Gothic Line—important German defensive line in northern Italy

Gunners—crew members of bomber aircraft

Haywire—not working correctly, crazy

Jerry—a German soldier or anything else German; originated in World War I but did not see common use until World War II

Joe—coffee

KIA—killed in action

Kraut—German; shortened from sauerkraut

Lay an egg—drop a bomb

Mickey Mouse movies—usually government-produced movies about personal hygiene

Mickey Mouse rules—useless rules

Million-dollar wound—a wound that is not life threatening but serious enough to send a soldier away from the fighting

Mortimer Snerd—a popular dummy created in 1938 by ventriloquist Edgar Bergen

Noncom/NCO—noncommissioned officer

Padre—chaplain

Pinup—poster of a beautiful girl to be pinned on the wall or in a locker; refer to Gibson Girls

POW—prisoner of war

Rear-echelon man—soldier assigned to military unit or headquarters far back from the front line; one concerned more with administration and supply

Roger—a response meaning all right or okay

Sand fly fever—disease that incapacitated large numbers of Allied soldiers, first noted in 1943 in areas of North Africa

Screaming meemies—small army rockets launched from the back of a jeep or truck, creating a frightening, high-pitched noise

SNAFU—situation normal, all f____ed up; refer to FUBAR

SPs—self-propelled artillery

Sweat it out—wait for something

That's all she wrote—sometimes said at the end of a mail call

That's for the birds—something meaningless

Trench mouth—severe infection of the gums, an ailment seen for centuries, first called this by soldiers in the trenches of World War I

Uncle Joe—Joseph Stalin

V-mail—Victory mail, postal system using paper and envelope in one piece to expedite service

Varga/Vargas Girls—pinups popular during World War II, created by Alberto Vargas and reproduced for inspiring the troops; seen almost everywhere, from magazines to soldiers' lockers to the noses of fighter airplanes

Vino—wine

Walkie-talkie—portable radio for sending and receiving information, usually used on the battlefield

Wilco/Roger Wilco—will comply, okay

Zipper pistols—Nazi machine guns

CHAPTER 14

The Fifth Army's 88th Infantry Division

Those Fighting Blue Devils

The 88th Infantry Division of the US Army was first organized in World War I. It was activated in August 1917 and arrived overseas from Iowa in early September 1918, near the end of the war. Comprising primarily National Guard units, the 88th participated in trench fighting in France. The division did not fight as a whole in major battles and so experienced relatively few casualties—a total reported to be under one hundred. At times its veteran units acted as support for other units during World War I. Commanders of the division included Generals Plummer, Getty, Beach, and Weigel. The division was deactivated in June 1919.

America entered World War II in December 1941, and July 1942 saw the reactivation of the Fifth Army's 88th Infantry Division at Camp Gruber, Oklahoma. This division was the first army division whose troops were created mostly from draftees. Prior to that, army divisions were filled by the Regular Army, the Reserves, or the National Guard. The untrained recruits faced a rigorous boot camp designed to toughen them up and train them to think more of their unit than of themselves. They quickly learned how to make their beds and clean their barracks, perform kitchen duty, march, drill, clean and fire their rifles, and endure the discipline of the military. They completed night marches and obstacle courses and learned how to put on gas masks and depend on each other. Additionally, training of officers—my father included—at Camp Gruber included technical courses, leadership training, problem solving, logistics, doctrine, and other specialized training.

After extensive training at Camp Gruber, the 88th moved to the Louisiana Maneuver Area in 1943, continuing their training in northern and central Louisiana at Fort Polk and nearby smaller camps. In late August 1943 the division moved to Fort Sam Houston in San Antonio, Texas. The division's arrival in San Antonio was lauded in local newspapers and among the citizenry with fanfare and patriotism.

After completing their training there, the soldiers departed Fort Sam Houston in November 1943 and headed by train to Camp Patrick Henry in Virginia. This was the division's designated POE—port of embarkation—to North Africa and points beyond.

By late December 1943, all three infantry regiments—the 349th, 350th, and 351st—of the 88th Infantry Division had arrived and assembled in North Africa. After being sent to various locations such as Oran for further training and acclimation, units then gathered in Naples, Italy, by mid- to late February 1944. Considered to be the first draftee division in a combat zone in Italy, if not all of Europe, the 88th saw some of the hardest, bloodiest battles of World War II. They engaged in two of the most difficult encounters in Italy, the battles of Mt. Battaglia and Mt. Cassino. Aptly nicknamed by some as the Battle Mountain Regiment, the 350th Regiment—to which my father was assigned—earned the Distinguished Unit Citation. Their part in taking Rome in June 1944 was heralded as a major victory in the Italian campaign. In his diary, my father called it the key objective of the whole Fifth Army at that time.

President Roosevelt and other Americans had originally been reluctant to engage in a campaign to take Italy and free it from Nazi control. Churchill called Italy "the soft underbelly of Europe" and encouraged Roosevelt to commit to such an endeavor. Once the campaign was agreed upon, support was fully given, and the Allies succeeded in clearing German forces from Europe's soft underbelly. This was a long, exhausting, and bloody campaign, though, and the Allies were still battling it out, far north across the Po Valley, when the Germans surrendered on May 2, 1945.

The 88th Infantry Division played a major role in the defeat of the German army in Italy. The division served some 344 days in combat and saw more than 2,200 men killed in action and more than 9,000 wounded. Finally, throughout the summer of war's end in Europe, many troops were able to return home. Some members of the division remained in Italy for a time, however, to help maintain peace and to guard German POWs. The 88th's final deactivation occurred in October 1947.

Although originally named the Clover Leaf Battalion because of the conspicuous blue cloverleaf patch on their uniforms, the 88th Division became known as the Fighting Blue Devils during the war. According to some sources, this name supposedly originated with German troops, who greatly respected the fighting ability of the 88th. During at least one altercation, the German forces' battleground loudspeakers purportedly boomed derogatory terms toward nearby US troops. In hopes of disheartening the American soldiers, the Germans called them devils as an insult; however, the division's troops liked this name and took it as their own.

Without a doubt and almost without exception, the soldiers of the 88th—my father included—felt immensely proud of belonging to the Fighting Blue Devils. Even after the war, the Blue Devils prized continued camaraderie. Dad visited and corresponded with numerous war buddies for years, many of whom he mentioned in his diary. He attended regular Blue Devil reunions throughout the years after the war. He served as an officer in their postwar groups and kept meticulous records of meetings. I was able to use these records to learn more about some Blue Devil descendants.

This photo shows only some of the uniform insignia my father wears at different times in the service.

CHAPTER 15

In the Words of Others

"Well, write me, what say?"

My father wrote constantly all his life and collected the written word in its many forms. He trimmed out quotes to tape on his desk for inspiration; he pored over local and regional newspapers; he organized and stored in nearly pristine condition the *Stars and Stripes*, *Yank* magazine, and later *Life* and *Time*. He collected antique publications and read them alongside current releases. Often on a lazy Sunday afternoon, or just about any late night after Mom had gone to bed, I could find him reading books or stacks of letters he had saved.

Combing through his boxes years later, I was surprised to find so many bundles of letters my dad had saved from the war. One of the large bundles that were clipped together held letters sent to him from war buddies, particularly later in the war. I find it difficult to imagine, in this day of text messages and emails, that letter writing was so frequent and important to the men, whether sent from the States or from the front.

Following are excerpts of just some of the communication my father saved from 1942 through 1945. Like my dad, I was gratified to see the concern and admiration that officers had for each other on the battlefield and off. Truly, comrades in arms. While these messages confirm my father's character as I knew him, they also picture for readers other unique, personal views of the war. The dates attributed to them are the dates that the letters were written rather than when they were postmarked, which could be days or weeks later.

Names that are included contextually or in closing signatures have occasionally been edited to preserve confidentiality, or because locating their descendants proved difficult. Also, in some cases, they simply were not legible.

As a side note, I did not expect to learn that some servicemen occasionally wrote to Alice, often mentioning their hopes that she would feel better. The tone in which they expressed their wishes for her seemed somewhat out of the ordinary. I wondered just how much my father had confided in his fellow officers about her health, or whether he had simply asked them to write to Alice to cheer her up.

Postcard from Fort Benning, Georgia, Wednesday, June 3, 1942

Dear Mrs. M:

Just a line to let you know old Bob is still hanging on. At the moment, he's having his locks trimmed in the barber chair and yours truly is waiting. We have hopes of graduating Thursday and I expect he'll be home to see you shortly thereafter.

Hope you're feeling much better.

"New Hamp" Lt. Willand

Letter dated December 23 [year is uncertain]

Dear Alice,

Your dear husband is one of the most virtuous men I have ever come in contact with. You should be proud of this grand man of yours.

Alice may God bless you and yours well and happy [*sic*].

With all that's within me I hope the day will come when we will be together again.

My very best to you.

Col. Lynch

Excerpt of letter from Camp Croft, South Carolina, Saturday, August 28, 1943

Dear Major Melcher,

Couldn't resist the pleasure of writing to my favorite Officer. Want to congratulate you on your recent and deserved promotion. Golly, G-3 had better watch out, for it wouldn't surprise me one bit if you become the 88th's Plans and Training Officer.

Can imagine how terribly sorry you are about staying at Houston. Texas and Melcher go like bread and butter. Do hope the blasted war is over before the 88th moves out, for it's bound to terminate once you get into action. . . . I was assigned to the 7th Regiment and last night assigned to Company C. Guess I'm here for a year or so now, but I'd rather be with a combat Division rather than an I.R.T.C. [Infantry Replacement Training Center] outfit. We teach basic here by committee, and last week I taught map reading and to my utmost surprise did a good job of it.

Remember how Captain Melcher always drew Bn. O.D. [battalion officer of the day] on Sundays? I'm getting my dose now, today and tomorrow. Best of luck to you, Major, and I want to add again that as an Officer and friend, you're tops.

Arch

Excerpt of letter, Friday, January 7, 1944

Dear Bob,

You need not have been so damn disrespectful in slinging that "sir" around in your letter—but after three days resting in [Italy] I can well imagine that you didn't know half what you were doing nor have cared if you did. [Knowing my "Uncle" Jack Miller, I think this was written in a joking manner. He and my dad were lifelong friends, starting as classmates at A&M and extending until Uncle Jack's passing in San Antonio at the age of sixty-two.]

It was really swell hearing from you and made me damned ashamed for not having kept my end of the correspondence up but so help me Hannah I won't slip from Grace again. Our bunch [of Aggies] has really scattered to hell and gone, but there will come that day when we will gather round the beer barrel and barbecue pit and swap lies, brother what a day that will be.

I am now A-1 of the 9th Bombardment Division somewheres [*sic*] in France and living in a manner to which I was never accustomed. The General for some reason took a shine to me so am doing okay if I can just keep my nose clean. I have more work to do than I can say Grace over and frankly a hell of a lot of it is too big for me, but I have some good people working for me.

You can be assured of a warm welcome ifn [*sic*] you can get loose from where you are. It would really be a good deal and I know we could find something for you to do. . . . Think there is a chance? If so, ask for a transfer and I'll fix this end when it gets to me. Hurry up and clean up that mess down there [in Italy] and come on up to our house.

Jack [Lt. Col. James Miller]

Headquarters 88th Infantry Division

United States Army

APO 88

AG 200.6

SUBJECT: Award of the Bronze Star Medal.

TO: Major Robert L. Melcher, 0294980, Infantry, G-3 Section, Headquarters

Replacement and Training Command, Mediterranean Theater of Operations.

CITATION

Robert L. Melcher, 0294980, Major, Infantry, G-3 Section, Headquarters Replacement and Training Command, Mediterranean Theater of Operations. For meritorious service in combat in Italy from 11 May 1944 to 1 December 1944. During this period, the 350th Infantry Regiment, of which Major MELCHER was then S-3, was almost constantly engaged with the enemy in heavy fighting through the mountains of Italy in an advance from the Garigliano River to the Northern Appenines [sic] region. Throughout the period, Major MELCHER performed his duties with minute attention to every detail, frequently spending long and tedious hours to insure the complete and thorough preparation of the Regiment's tactical plans. Under the most adverse conditions, exposed to artillery and mortar fire on hundreds of occasions, without adequate rest or food, Major MELCHER always gave of his best services, and is deserving of lasting credit for his share in the victorious achievement of American arms. His services were particularly important and valuable in the successful attacks of the Regiment at Mt. Cianelli, Roccasecca, Volterra and Mt. Battaglia. His conduct on the field of battle always reflected great credit upon himself and was in keeping with the glorious traditions of the American infantry. Entered military service from La Grange, Texas.

J. C. Fry

Brigadier General,

U.S. Army, Commanding.

Above and facing, This Bronze Star is one of the few war relics Dad shows me when I am growing up. He says little about it, but I know it is important to him. I rediscover it many years later.

BRONZE STAR
MEDAL

Excerpt of letter, Monday, May 29, 1944

Dear Bob,

Tho't I'd drop you a few lines, . . . just to let you know down deep from the bottom of my heart, the big factor you contributed to the success of the Fighting 350th.

You were loyal, energetic, trustworthy and an asset to any command.

I will always regret the day when I had to leave such a grand and loyal bunch of troops. . . .

Sincerely, Col. Pete

Excerpt of letter from "Sunny Italy," Wednesday, June 28, 1944

Dearest Alice,

Bob is busy working so he asked me to write you a letter for him, but if I'm going to write 'twill be for myself and not for him. . . .

I have thought of you so very often and, through Bob, have known that you were getting along as well as most of our war widows. . . .

Bob and I thought we were young again this afternoon so we got a football from the recreation tent and proceeded to have us a football game. We do not expect to be able to move tomorrow but we did have fun while it lasted. You'd be surprised what relaxation it is to get to do something like that so you can forget the war for a while. Bob is getting along great. Don't worry about him, we'll take care of him and before you can count ten, we'll be walking down the gang planks in some port in the good old U.S.A.

Sincerely, Collier

Excerpt of letter, Saturday, September 16, 1944

Dear Bob,

Just a line to say hello, and to let you know that I'm improving stedely [*sic*]. Am able to walk again—some, but not good. As you know, I received a hell of a lick in my legs. It almost cut the big tendon under my right knee in two. They will probably send me back to duty in a month or so, but I feel that it will be a long time before I can take the mountains and rugged marches as I used to.

Well, Bob, how are things going with you and the rest of the 350th? I understand you had a good rest this last time. Would like to hear from the outfit more often just to keep in contact with it. The only news that gets back here [2628 Hospital Section] is usually printed in the Stars & Stripes. And by the way, could you give me the low down on this citation or award or whatever it is that I received and what for? Damn if I can figure it out. Well, write me, what say?

Griff

Excerpt of letter, Friday, October 20, 1944

Dear Bob,

Thanks a million for your letter dated 9 October which arrived yesterday. It was just heap full of the kind of news I've been wanting.

My heart went sick though when I read of the many KIAs among the Officers who gave their very best to make the 350th the grand fighting outfit it is. You know what my contribution always was. I'll regret the rest of my life that I didn't hang on. I might have been able to pull through in spite of my bad knee. It still gives me a little trouble but I have some good fighting days left in me and it won't be long before you're hearing from me again. I'll be meeting you all some time before this show is over, mark my words.

. . . It goes without saying that I always had the greatest of admiration for each and every one of you. Who the hell raised you all, and picked the staff who have done the magnificent job that you have?

Maybe some day I can rejoice and help share in the glory that every member of our outfit is entitled to. I feel that you all still belong to me and that I belong to you.

. . . May God bless and bring you all back home.

Col. Pete

Excerpt of letter, Sunday, December 10, 1944

Major Melcher:

I thought you might like to have a copy of the memorandum authorizing you another battle star. Some of us sure miss you and hope you are having a grand rest and a complete change from the strain you have worked under. With the exception of a few shells coming in, things are quiet here.

Lewis

Excerpt of letter, Saturday, December 23, 1944

Dear Bob,

This is Christmas time and at this time of the year, we should all be happy and that's what we wish for you here in the S-1 Section . . . you have been a great inspiration and example to us and to the other officers and men of this Regiment. We want you to know that whether you stay in Italy or whether you go home, we profoundly feel that you belong to us.

There's not a lot going on here. However, it is rather cold. I'm looking out the window—I can see a few flakes of snow falling that seem to carry the promise of a white Christmas. I haven't been feeling too well for almost a week. However, I am generally happy, even in all this, possibly because when I was very young, my mother taught me that everything happens for the best.

Lt. Smith just came in and wanted to convey the best wishes and sincerest greetings for the Officers of Headquarters Company. We all want you to know that wherever you are and whatever you are doing that we're for you.

Joe M______

[Note: Eight other officers' signatures are added to the close of this Christmas message.]

Excerpt of letter, Tuesday, January 16, 1945

Dear Sir:

. . . Let me pay you a couple of compliments and it is not brown nosing. You are one of the men that I want to meet [meet up with] when this mess is over. Everybody that knows you always says what a fine gentleman you are. They always ask for you and want to know if you are coming back. This is my wish that you don't come back: I hope you get a job counting empty beer bottles or maybe running a rest camp. If you do get a job like this please let the other fellow do his share. That is your biggest fault—you try to do everything yourself.

Collier

Excerpt of letter, Wednesday, February 7, 1945

Dear Sir:

. . . We sit around and pray that the Russians make it [to Berlin] this time. The only one missing now is Major Collier. He is sick and we don't expect him back for at least ten more days. . . . Capt. F______ has been doing a good

HEADQUARTERS 350TH INFANTRY
APO #88, U. S. ARMY

23 December 1944.

Dear Bob:

This is Christmas time and at this time of the year, we should all be happy and that's what we wish for you here in the S-1 Section. Mr. Matthias and I both miss you a great deal, for in all earnestness, we both feel that you have been a great inspiration and example to us and to the other officers and men of this Regiment. We want you to know that whether you stay in Italy or whether you go home, we profoundly feel that you belong to us.

There's not a lot going on here, however, it is rather cold. I'm looking out the window - I can see a few flakes of snow falling that seem to carry the promise of a white Christmas. I haven't been feeling too well for almost a week, however, I am generally happy, even in all this, possibly because when I was very young, my mother taught me that everything happens for the best.

Lieutenant Smith just came in and wanted to convey the best wishes and sincerest greetings for the officers of Headquarters Company. We all want you to know that wherever you are and whatever you are doing that we're for you.

Sincerely,

JOE V. MCREY,
Captain, Infantry,
Adjutant.

Christmas wishes and compliments are sent to my father, hospitalized at the 64th General Hospital after being moved from the 56th Evacuation Hospital.

job but last night against my advice he got involved in a pick and shovel deal. I had told him it was a job for the S-4 and he ought to mind his own business. He had picks and shovels on one end, guides on the wrong end, and the truck driver was not so bright. I finally got him out of the mess and everything on its way. Well, the last straw was when they called him up and told him that he did not send the correct number of shovels. Write to me and let me know where you are because one of these days I am going to try for a pass and I will try to see you.

Costello

Excerpt of letter, Thursday, February 8, 1945

My dear Major,

I went down to the 64th yesterday and was very sorry to have missed you. But I am delighted to know that you have improved to the place where you can leave the hospital. I have wanted to get over there for quite a while but my jeep has been in ordnance for about a month. I got it out only recently. . . . I am now at the Rest Center on a duty status for 10 days.

Major, we miss you up yonder very much. I have heard so many fine things about you and your work. . . . If I can be of any service to you up here, don't hesitate to call on the best Chaplain in the US Army!

Henry Pressly

Excerpt of letter, Sunday, March 18, 1945

. . . We have had two campaigns and out of about 25 Officers that came over [to the Pacific theater of war] with me out of the 88th, we have very few left. In fact very few and Ray B______ is the only one promoted. About half of your recent letter was blacked out.

. . . I've seen hundreds of the Filipinos starved to death with their hands tied behind their backs—nuns bayoneted—babies too—well anything you read about the [enemy] you can multiply 100 times and that won't start to show you how mean and cruel they are. . . . So you see there is no quitting here. They don't get captured and we don't either. This is really total war. No give and take. I've lain out six days with dead all around me but no one called a truce to bury anybody's dead. . . .

F______

Excerpt of letter, Wednesday, May 30, 1945

Dear Major Bob,

We missed you this last push in case you already didn't know it. This country we are located in [Cavalese, Italy] now is quite beautiful. We are all more or less sweating it out. Nobody knows whether we will go direct to the Pacific or not. It wouldn't be so bad if they would send us by way of the states. . . .

This is a liberated kraut typewriter so you will have to excuse the mistakes. We also acquired a beautiful radio. During the push McD______ and myself were presented with another radio by the people of Nogara for liberating their city. There were krauts all over the place. I captured 9 myself and believe it or not the S-1 section [Personnel] even got a few.

We would appreciate the opportunity of seeing you again. Trust we may be that lucky. In any event, we would appreciate hearing from you soon and often.

Dan W______

Afterword

1945 to the Present

"May your words live on."

My father spent nineteen-plus months overseas with the 88th Infantry Division as a battalion officer and regiment operations officer in G-3 (Training and Operations). He finished the war in Italy as a major with two Bronze Stars (I could find only one, but he mentioned two in some of his papers) and other awards. He returned to his home state of Texas in July 1945, thanking God for his good fortune. Dad was urged by his commanding officer and others to reenlist full time in the Regular Army, but he chose civilian life instead, eventually transitioning to the Army Reserve, to live again the good life in Texas with his adored wife, Alice.

How people can change, though, with wartime's effects and reacquaintance with each other after returning home. Sadly, divorce followed in 1948 for my dad and Alice. I know very little about the nature of their divorce. He never talked to me about it, and my mom was short on words as well. I remember asking Mom about a lady named Alice, after a schoolmate had announced to me on the playground that my father had been married before. ("Liar!" I had responded at the time.) Mom briefly informed me about the first marriage and said it had ended because of Alice's mental state, giving a few secondhand anecdotes. I always sensed my mother's resentment of his marriage to Alice and of the fact that many of Dad's coworkers on campus had known her.

At the time of their divorce in 1948, my father was back in College Station and had been named assistant commandant of the Corps of Cadets at Texas A&M. His summers included Reserve duty, usually at Fort Sam Houston in San Antonio. It was there in 1949 that his brother Max, also on Reserve duty, introduced him to an attractive young secretary at the post, Glyn Etta Gilpin Goddard.

Herself newly single, Glyn Etta radiated beauty, good health, and youthfulness, being some fifteen years younger than Dad. For him, she was a breath of fresh air. What fun they had! A whirlwind romance ensued that summer of 1949, and in August they married in a short ceremony at her parents' home in San Antonio. Dad introduced Glyn to College Station, and they began their new life there that autumn. Dad's quarters at the Fish Annex—a freshman campus outside town—quickly proved insufficient. They felt that their home there would be too small for what they hoped would be a growing family. Mom and Dad built a new home that still stands today in town. I was born a year later, their only child, in the autumn of 1950, and we lived there on Ashburn Drive until the early 1960s when they built a larger, more modern home several blocks away.

Dad continued his service to his country in the Army Reserve. His assignments included numerous summer tours. I remember fondly the summers he served in San Antonio at Fort Sam Houston, because we often went with him and lived on post or at my grandparents' house. At times my Uncle Max and his family were assigned there during the summer, too. We cousins played on post while our moms visited, shopped downtown, or spent time in their homes.

Dad retired as a colonel to inactive Reserve in 1962, and he was formally retired from the army in 1970. In the mid-1970s, he retired from Texas A&M University, where he had worked as assistant commandant of the Corps, international student adviser, and administrative officer in the Dean of Students Office. Throughout his career at the university, he worked to help students achieve success. Dad remained close to many students and their families long after their graduation, and he saved numerous letters from them. He was recognized through the years with numerous honors for his service to students, and he proudly received Texas A&M's Distinguished Faculty Achievement Award in 1976.

My mother, Glyn Etta Gilpin Goddard, is photographed circa 1949, around the time she meets my father on post in San Antonio.

In these postwar years, my father enjoyed much that he had dreamed about while he was overseas: a satisfying career helping others; glorious days hunting and fishing in Central Texas; Aggie football in the stands. He thanked God for being able to live the dream life he had longed to return to after the war. Dad cherished once again living in his home state and continuing the Melcher family's German traditions that he loved, surrounded by family and friends. He lived to do right by his fallen comrades in Italy, just as he had once written in his war diary, and he was known for his dedication to helping A&M students.

Most likely from the day I was born, Dad never missed a chance to teach me to "do the right thing" and to "finish what you start." He valued hard work, honesty, courage, loyalty, and decency, and he instilled these values into my life as well. (Dad also taught me phrases in German, which I found to be fun even though I never spoke the language around my friends.) He was a sociable man whose door was always open. He and my mother remained close to many of his college and army buddies, some of whom had returned or relocated to College Station. With others living elsewhere, my father maintained regular communication through letters (another bundle of letters that I found) and occasional reunions.

Ever the patriot, my father passed away on Flag Day in June 1991. My mother remained in the family home they had designed and built together in the 1960s, where I had grown up in College Station. Mom lived on Francis Drive in comfort, enjoying visiting with her two grandsons, Thomas and Ryan, and still rooting for all things Aggie. She maintained a relatively active lifestyle, particularly busying herself with the Daughters of the Republic of Texas and other genealogical groups. All the while, she watched as her little pond and the nearby woods were encroached on by the growing suburbs. And then it was time for Mom to move to assisted living.

Summer 2011 found me cleaning out the family home to help Mom prepare for her move. One day, my project included tackling the den's large bookcases. I packed up her books and decor from each shelf. Next, I opened the overfull cabinets underneath. The cabinets' interiors looked as if Mom had not touched their contents since Dad's passing. Behind file folders and containers of old coins and stamps, I discovered dusty scrapbooks, magazines, maps, and yellowed letters, still bound together with brittle rubber bands.

For the first time, I saw my father's small, black-covered war diary.

Sweating and hurrying to finish emptying the den so I could drive home to Houston, I could little afford the time to sit down and rest, much less start reading Dad's diary. I was tired, and moving Mom across town and selling the house were the immediate priorities that hung over my head. I added Dad's memories to yet another jumbled box or three from the garage and sealed them up.

I'll read all of this someday when I have time, I promised myself.

The next four years flew by. Mom grew accustomed to life in assisted living, and I was busy with my own life in Houston. We visited, though, by daily phone calls or my driving to see her. We still loved to shop together. Mom was still my favorite shopping buddy, even when encumbered with her bulky wheelchair.

Mom passed away in May 2015. That summer, once again I found myself cleaning out and sorting through my mother's belongings. I even found boxes stashed under Mom's bed that I had packed four years earlier, still unopened. Many of the possessions from her apartment in assisted living were donated or given to her caretakers and friends; some items went to a local antiques auction; others made their way to my husband's and my home in Houston. Conserving space inside our home was starting to be an issue—like my father, I too was a collector of antiques and assorted ephemera—so most of what I had inherited had to be stored in boxes at the side of our garage.

Almost out of sight, almost out of mind.

Those dusty old boxes kept staring at me. Months later, I dragged myself out to our sweltering garage and set about sorting through them. Eventually, I reorganized, refilled, and labeled—with my own careful, distinctive lettering that was much like Dad's—numerous cartons and bins. Some contained family photos dating back to the early 1800s. Others harked back to my parents' early years together. Some boasted college souvenirs from 1928 to 1932, including Dad's college scrapbooks and even the Old Sarge college pennant he had once pinned to his dorm room wall. Still more boxes stored decorative items Mom had loved so much that I could not bring myself to give them away. How could I have delayed this task for so long?

The box ordeal, as I had come to regard it, lasted several months, with warm memories and a few tears as my companions. I remember the day I started tackling the very last boxes. Incredibly, their tape had held well; still sealed, untouched, inside each box lay the war memorabilia I had randomly packed and quickly disregarded in 2011. But I was tired this day, too.

I'll read all of this someday when I have time, I promised myself.

My dad and I had always been close. Strict and hard to fool—German strict, intelligence officer omniscient—he was, but he was also the teacher and encourager of my life. Why, then, did I continually delay reading what Dad had kept for so long? I remembered hearing Dad's war stories, of course, but this face-to-face encounter with his reality was proving too emotional. I still was not sure I was ready to meet my dad in his former life, in his own words. Perhaps I feared experiencing his thoughts and trials as a young impressionable soldier in battle. Would I see his frailty as a human being?

By late 2017, my excuses had run out. It was time to read Dad's war memories and learn about the young man I had never known. I opened his diary. Soon I was devouring pages filled with his distinctive, careful handwriting that I remembered so well.

I felt strangely comforted.

A window opened.

For the first time in my life, I saw my father as a young man—and I saw a man's heart that I already knew, that I already respected and loved. Here was a young soldier with longings and fears, questions about humanity, love of his country and family. Here too was a man with an undying faith.

I already knew this man! For the first time since he had passed, I could hear Dad speaking.

I kept my promise to myself. I read it all.

I felt that my dad's memories of the war should be shared, so I decided in 2018 to make copies of his war diary to hand down to my two sons. This would make a good Christmas gift for them, I thought. Scanning their grandfather's diary into the computer proved less than satisfactory because his penciled pages had faded too much. The solution was transcribing Dad's writing onto the computer, typing that took me untold hours, often late at night. Reading more than one hundred personal letters from his war years, I knew that some of those should be included in the project too.

As time went on, I uncovered even more of Dad and Alice's scrapbooks. They yielded numerous photos, clippings, and other relics he had saved in his footlocker or sent home to Alice. I should capture images of some of these, as well.

Dad's project grew. Delving deeper into his war years demanded researching many of the details in his diary. I studied books, magazine and newspaper articles, army orders and monthly reports. I followed links, requested records, viewed maps with troop movements, and corresponded with people from my parents' past. Many sources confirmed countless details that my dad had entered into his diary and written in his letters. I was impressed by his correct recounting of events—and I was surprised at his admission of increasing battle weariness and doubts. Supposedly, the army's postal censors

Dad carefully pastes photo after photo in scrapbooks after the war.

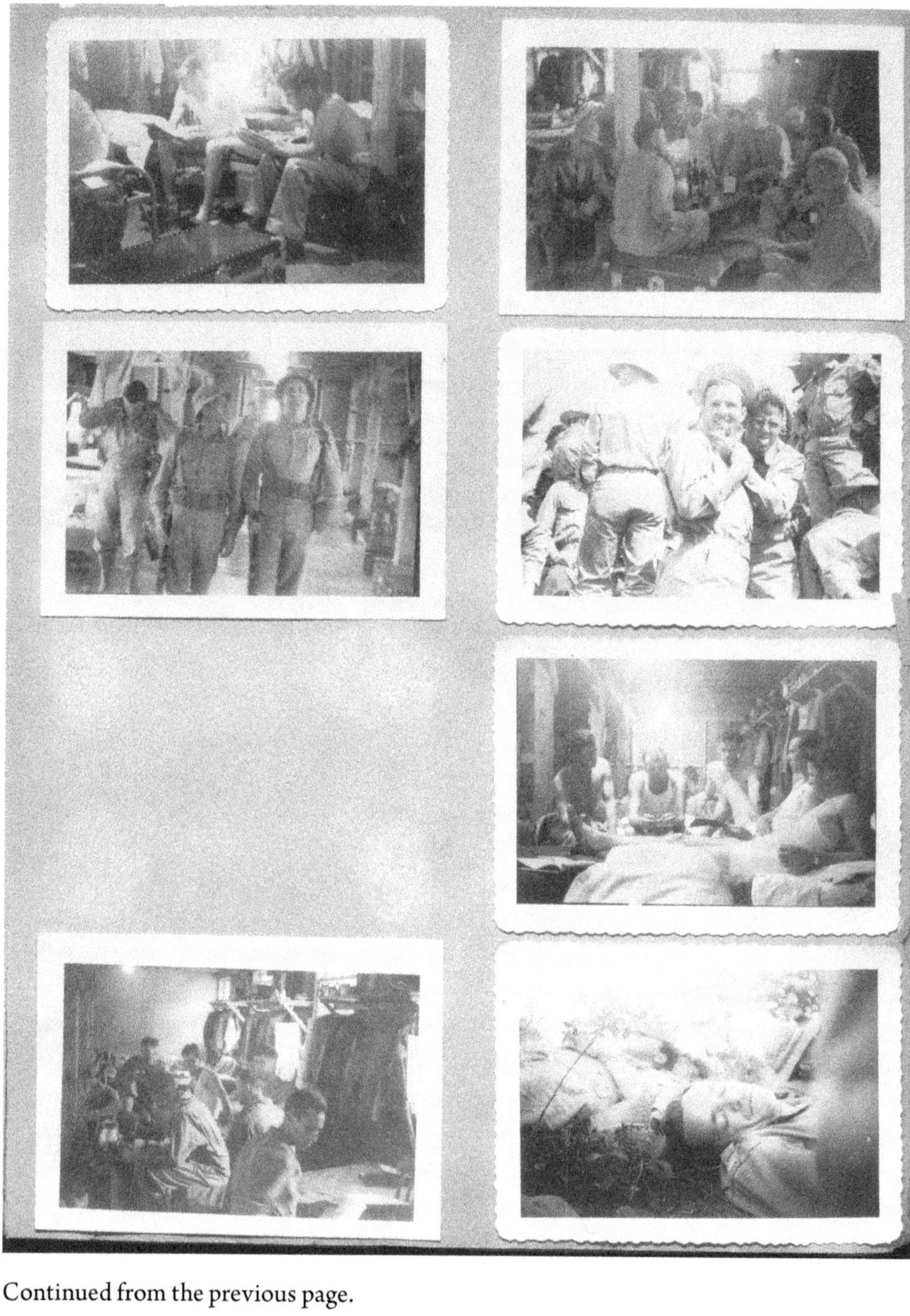

Continued from the previous page.

read all communications going to or coming from home. I wondered that they did not censor soldiers' diaries as well, unless it was because they had been so well hidden.

Surprisingly, as I read through the diary, I also discovered sources of bits and pieces of family lore. I had always heard about "Melcher luck," and I was surprised to see that my dad had mentioned it in a 1944 letter to his mother. As a child I had heard the story about Dad's being fired at while "visiting" a latrine, and he had written about that in his diary. I even found a hand-drawn cartoon created by one of the men to depict this occurrence.

Today, only a few questions remain. Dad's writings about Alice and the five or six pictures he had saved of her finally revealed some details about the woman I had only briefly heard about from Mom—never from Dad. I could see what she had looked like, but why had so little from Alice been saved? I found just one brief letter, a few cards, and that sealed envelope containing Texas dirt. What had precipitated their divorce in 1948? All I knew came from the divorce decree itself: incompatibility. Even though my parents met several years after the divorce and had a long and comfortably loving relationship, I sensed that Mom always harbored a little resentment toward Dad's tender, all-consuming first love. Perhaps she had read my father's wartime diary and had chosen not to tell me much about Alice. Could she have destroyed Alice's correspondence? Or had my father, long ago, in the throes of divorce?

I wondered too about my father's emotional and physical struggles near the end of the war. His relentless personal battles must have been similar to those of some other war-weary soldiers in our country's history. Not just World War II, but Korea, Vietnam, Afghanistan, and Iraq, in more recent years, came to mind. Thankfully, Dad's difficulties were addressed during the war, and at least he was able to write about them. Dad never told me about his issues, though. He continued to experience headaches and sleep difficulties off and on for the rest of his life. Could these have been part of his own version of what is known today as PTSD—post-traumatic stress disorder?

Ultimately, what began as a collection of a grandfather's war memories ended up as this book, taking more than five years to complete. During the process, Dad's memoir proved more than ever that the hero of my youth was in reality not *less* of a hero but *more*. Certainly as a young man he was afraid and vulnerable at times. Even then, though, just as I knew him, he was also a tender-hearted, hardworking, loyal American who trusted in God.

He reconciled his hard feelings toward the Germans—the Nazis—with his memories of growing up in a loving German Texan family and community. He continued to love his family's traditions and passed those down to me. He was always ready to lend an ear or help someone in need, and he was respected by those around him. I had known Dad to be this way throughout his lifetime, and I learned that this was my father as a young man, too. Consistent to the end, Dad was an exemplary role model.

I found answers to my father's—and my—past.

I hope that my father's words can challenge others—even if but one life—today, to live with "honesty and courage and decency."

Thanks, Dad. May your words live on.

I remember my father wearing this officer's hat when he had Reserve duty. It is still in excellent shape from being carefully protected through the years.

My father, "The Colonel," poses for the camera in his Reserve officer's uniform.

ACKNOWLEDGMENTS

First, appreciation goes to my father, who saved everything, who encouraged my creativity from an early age, and who taught me the value—and sometimes the pain—of finishing what I start.

Thanks and love go to my husband, Steven, for his eternal patience with my never-ending questions and for his inspired, sensitive reading and suggestions along the way.

For the intelligent critiquing of the manuscript, and guidance toward publication, I thank my mentor and author John Adams. For reading a very rough first draft, I appreciate my cousin Col. Max D. Melcher (US Army, Retired), and my sister-in-law Sondra Kreiner. Thanks also go to copyeditor Laurel Anderton for her careful, thoughtful suggestions. Finally, publication would not have been possible without the help of the staff at Texas A&M University Press, including Thom Lemmons and Abagail Chartier.

Thank you, too, reader, for indulging me in my efforts to honor my father and to learn more about his legacy.

SELECTED BIBLIOGRAPHY

Sources used by the author include but are not limited to the following.

"88th Infantry Division." MtMestas.com. Continually updated. https://mtmestas.com/

"88th Infantry Division Moves to Fort Sam after Completing Maneuvers in Louisiana." *San Antonio Evening News*, 2 September 1943.

Alexander, Christine, and Mason Kunze. *Eastern Inferno: The Journals of a German Panzerjäger on the Eastern Front, 1941–1943*. Havertown, PA: Casemate Publishers, 2010.

"Allied Armies Smash Inland on Broad Front in Normandy." *Houston Chronicle*, 6 June 1944.

Atkinson, Rick. *The Day of Battle: The War in Sicily and Italy*. New York: Henry Holt, 2007.

Beltz, April Martin. *Letters across the Pacific: A Love Story in the Time of War*. BookLocker, 2020.

Brister, Louis E. "Adelsverein." Texas Historical Association. Updated 25 August 2018. https://www.tshaonline.org/handbook/entries/adelsverein

Bryan, Jami. "The 88th Infantry Division in Italy." Army Historical Foundation. 20 January 2015. https://armyhistory.org/the-88th-infantry-division-in-italy/

Dillon, Eva. *Spies in the Family: An American Spymaster, His Russian Crown Jewel, and the Friendship That Helped End the Cold War*. New York: HarperCollins, 2017.

Ehrlich, Paul. "World War I in West Texas: The Tar and Feathering of a Texas Priest." Texas Hill Country. 31 December 2020. https://texashillcountry.com/tar-feathering-texas-priest/

"Florence American Cemetery Overview." American Battle Monuments Commission. Updated 1 April 2022. https://www.abmc.gov/Florence

Gann, Harvey E. *Escape I Must! World War II Prisoner of War in Germany.* Austin, TX: Woodburner Press, 2013.

Guide for Participants in Peace, Stability, and Relief Operations. United States Institute of Peace. 15 June 2007. https://www.usip.org/publications/2007/06/guide-participants-peace-stability-and-relief-operations

Hughes, Thomas A., and John Graham Royde-Smith. "World War II, 1939–1945." Brittanica. 20 September 2019. https://www.britannica.com/event/World-War-II

"Italian Campaign." History.com. Updated 2019. https://www.history.com/topics/world-war-ii/italian-campaign

"It's All Over Here." *Stars and Stripes Mediterranean,* 8 May 1945.

Jordan, Terry G. "Germans." Texas Historical Association. Updated 29 November 2019. https://www.tshaonline.org/handbook/entries/germans

Ketcher, Chad. "Friendships That Outlive War." *Texas Hill Country Culture* 4, no. 11 (November 2019): 28–29.

Koehler, Franz A. *Special Rations for the Armed Forces, 1946–53.* QMC Historical Studies, series 2, no. 6. Washington, DC: Historical Branch, Office of the Quartermaster General, 1958.

"K-ration." Wikimedia Foundation. Updated 18 October 2023. https:/en.wikipedia.org/wiki/K-ration

Laurie, Clayton D. "Rome-Arno 1944." U.S. Army Center of Military History. 3 October 2003. https://www.history.army.mil/brochures/romar/72-20.htm

Lomax, John Nova. "Sprechen Sie Texas Deutsch? How a Variation of German Once Ruled in Fredericksburg." *Texas Highways,* 1 June 2021.

Malanowski, Jamie. "Vivat, Vivat Varga Girl!" *Esquire,* November 1994.

McKay, Brett, and Kate McKay. "Blow It Out Your Barracks Bag: WWII Slang from the Front." Art of Manliness. Updated 25 October 2020. https://www.artofmanliness.com/character/military/wwii-slang/

Melcher, Robert Lee. "Some Information about Grandpa Melcher." 4 May 1969. Personal papers.

Milzarski, Eric. "This Is What the Army's Nasty 'Emergency Chocolate Bars' Tasted Like." We Are the Mighty. 29 April 2020. https://www.wearethemighty.com/mighty-history/field-ration-d-hersheys-chocolate/

My Life in the Service. Chicago: Consolidated Book Publishers, 1941.

Reilly, William A., MD, Roberto F. Escamilla, MD, and Perrin H. Long, MD. "Sandfly Fever." Chap. 2 in *Internal Medicine in World War II*, vol. 2. Washington, DC: Office of the Surgeon General. https://achh.army.mil/history/book-wwii-infectiousdisvolii-chapter2

Romeiser, John B., ed. *Combat Reporter: Don Whitehead's World War II Diary and Memoirs*. New York: Fordham University Press, 2006.

Smith, Gary. MtMestas.com. 2019. https://mtmestas.com/

Tippens, Matthew D. *Turning Germans into Texans: World War I and the Assimilation and Survival of German Culture in Texas, 1900–1930*. Kleingarten Press, 2010.

Tyler, Carol. *Soldier's Heart: The Campaign to Understand My WWII Veteran Father*. Seattle: Fantagraphics Books, 2015.

INDEX

© MK Photography

ABOUT THE AUTHOR

Marilyn Melcher Maddox has written across numerous disciplines, taught teachers how to teach the gifted and talented, and stood ready as a Phone a Friend. She grew up listening to Melcher family legends and lore, writing in her own diaries with typical teenage angst, and attending Texas Aggie football games from the tender age of one year.

Inspired at an early age by her father, Maddox learned to love the social sciences, and her interests naturally evolved into her first career as a secondary educator. Maddox was a Distinguished Graduate and Who's Who of Texas A&M University and enjoyed many years teaching at the secondary level. Not surprisingly, her favorite subjects to teach were history and language arts.

After retiring from education, Maddox built websites, wrote articles for trade magazines, and managed public relations for interior designers and stores in Houston, Texas. She published magazine articles on topics as wide ranging as practices in education (curriculum and instruction), employee relations, antiques, interior design, and home building. Ultimately, Maddox turned to fulfilling a dream: compiling her father's wartime memoir to pass along to his two grandsons, her sons Thomas and Ryan Atlee. What began as a simple project ultimately grew into this, her debut nonfiction book.

Now semiretired, Maddox spends her free time writing, volunteering, and selling American and European antiques. She returned in May 2021 to her hometown of College Station, Texas, where she is enjoying life with her very patient husband and two all-American West Highland White Terriers.

www.ingramcontent.com/pod-product-compliance
Lightning Source LLC
LaVergne TN
LVHW010726280825
819315LV00002B/4
* 9 7 8 1 6 4 8 4 3 3 3 2 0 *